Beryl McBurnie

THE CARIBBEAN BIOGRAPHY SERIES

The Caribbean Biography Series from the University of the West Indies Press celebrates and memorializes the architects of Caribbean culture. The series aims to introduce general readers to those individuals who have made sterling contributions to the region in their chosen field – literature, the arts, politics, sports – and are the shapers and bearers of Caribbean identity.

Other Titles in This Series

Earl Lovelace, by Funso Aiyejina
Derek Walcott, by Edward Baugh
Marcus Garvey, by Rupert Lewis

BERYL McBURNIE

Judy Raymond

The University of the West Indies Press
Jamaica • Barbados • Trinidad and Tobago

The University of the West Indies Press
7A Gibraltar Hall Road, Mona
Kingston 7, Jamaica
www.uwipress.com

A catalogue record of this book is
available from the National Library of Jamaica.
ISBN: 978-976-640-678-3 (cloth)
978-976-640-700-1 (paper)
978-976-640-679-0 (Kindle)
978-976-640-680-6 (ePub)

Cover photograph: Carl Van Vechten, *Belle Rosette in
African Costume* (slide no. 253, 1941), © Van Vechten Trust.
Beinecke Library, Yale University.
Reproduced by kind courtesy of the Carl Van Vechten Trust.

Jacket and book design by Robert Harris
Set in Whitman 11.5/15

Printed in the United States of America

For my children and their children, my grandfather
Arthur Raymond and my splendid aunts
Louise, Yvonne and Ursula

CONTENTS

INTRODUCTION

Tucked down a quiet side street in Woodbrook, in western Port of Spain, Trinidad, stands the only memorial to the woman who single-handedly rescued and revived West Indian folk dance from ignominy and oblivion.

A small, angular white building, it opens directly onto the pavement of Roberts Street, a narrow cross-street usually crammed with parked cars. Number 95 occupies a lot intended for a small family home, which is exactly what it housed until Beryl McBurnie made other plans for it almost a century ago: one day, she decided, this would be the site of the Little Carib Theatre.

In the opening-night programme of the theatre in 1948, future prime minister Dr Eric Williams wrote: "It is people like Beryl McBurnie who will improve conditions in the West Indies and upon whom more than anything else the future of the West Indies will depend." Today, a lifetime later, all that many people know of her is that she founded the Little Carib Theatre – but not the significance of the building or what happened there.

McBurnie herself was modest about what she personally had accomplished, but she knew the work was important. "I'm very interested in the classics; nothing can be more beautiful than *Tristan und Isolde*, nothing. But," she went on passionately, "you can't give a little girl an aria from the *Meistersingers* to sing in a competition for her country when there's a gallery of folk songs or even calypso, can you?" (Judy Raymond, "Lady of the Big Idea", *Sunday Express*, 17 October 1993, sect. 2, 1). She explained her life's work in another interview, in her sixties, dressed – costumed – in one of her usual eye-catching outfits: a white full-length flounced dress with lace at the wrists, topped with a colourful headwrap and overskirt (a version of the Martiniquan-style *douillette* worn to dance the belé). In her cut-glass diction, she recalled what had motivated her to return to the Caribbean after several years of studying and performing successfully in the United States. She described her own early, colonial education in dance: "We would be dancing nothing Trinidadian, nothing West Indian. The coloured child in dance or theatre was never really thought about, and something had to be done. What happened with me – it emerged, really; I didn't set out to make a political question of it; it just happened naturally."[1]

McBurnie was visionary, charismatic, charming, knowledgeable, driven, persistent and inspiring, but she did not achieve everything she set out to do, though today's Little Carib Theatre is grand compared with the original. Her determination led McBurnie to build it in the face of major obstacles, among them lack of funds and frequent threats of demolition. That same stubbornness kept her from allowing the theatre to evolve beyond her own personal vision – although a company had been set up to run the theatre, and she was just one of several people who had a say in it. The theatre companies that used to share the space have moved on, including the Trinidad Theatre Workshop, founded here by Nobel laureate Derek Walcott in the late 1950s. As for the Little Carib Dance Company, it ceased to exist long before her death.

In October 2016, McBurnie's second attempt to further her life's work, the Folk House, literally crumbled into dust, demolished at the behest of its new owners ("Home of Little Carib Founder Demolished", *Sunday Guardian*, 18 September 2016). The building, a few blocks west of the theatre, was her own home, but she had tried to make it into a training centre for the arts.[2]

Just as the Folk House is gone, so are the dances McBurnie created. As Rex Nettleford wrote, "Dance is among the most ephemeral of the arts, and dance companies are fragile plants that require patient and sensitive nurturing to survive."[3]

But McBurnie's work was not in vain. It continues through the many theatre companies, actors, dancers, musicians, folk-dance groups, and other visual and literary artists who discovered and honed their talents at the Little Carib. Her influence was felt across the region and beyond. Her name still appears on the website of Teachers College, Columbia University, in New York, where she briefly studied dance education in the 1930s (www.tc.columbia.edu/danceed/). She was honoured regionally and internationally. Little Carib dancers formed their own companies locally or went on to star overseas. Locally, folk-dance traditions are now maintained not only by semi-professional, trained dance companies, but also by the community groups that perform in the Prime Minister's Best Village competition every year. McBurnie lives on too through other artists who got their start at the Little Carib, whether playing steelpan, singing or designing Carnival costumes; and those in and from Trinidad and Tobago, other islands and far away who were inspired by her to start dance and theatre companies of their own.

Beryl McBurnie's life's work was to give West Indian people back to themselves. This book sets out to tell who she was, why she persevered in the task she set herself, and what she accomplished in her long, often seemingly thankless decades of dedication to Caribbean culture.

ONE

According to an anecdote Beryl McBurnie told in later years, as a young girl of about seven or eight she was invited to recite a poem, "The Sycamore Tree", for a charity concert at her school. She enjoyed it so much that she and her friends set up their own "Coralita Club" to organize a performance in her house. It rained that day, so no one came, but the cast sold the ice cream intended as refreshments for the audience, and McBurnie rescheduled the show – though this time her mother insisted it take place in the back yard. Entitled *Twinkling Lights*, it featured Beryl dancing to "The Beautiful Lady in Blue" and doing an Argentine tango.

This childhood remembrance almost sums up her life. The centre of her universe was the site of her family home at 95 Roberts Street, Woodbrook, Port of Spain, which since 1948 has been the site of the Little Carib Theatre; McBurnie spent much of her long life organizing performances on that very spot.[4]

McBurnie was by no means the only musical or adventurous member of the family. The house belonged to her mother's people, the Rollocks. Their family tree traces them back to Abel Skinner Rollock, aide-de-camp to Prince William Henry, younger brother of George III and captain of HMS *Pegasus* in the West Indies from 1786 to 1788 under Horatio Nelson. Rollock settled in Barbados, where he bought the Chance Hall estate and married an Englishwoman. He continued sailing with his family, but they all drowned at sea, except his baby son, who shared his name. Washed up on shore in Montserrat, the boy was identified and sent home to Barbados, but by then the overseer had sold the family estate, and Abel Rollock Junior eventually became a tailor to earn his liveli-hood. He married a coloured (mixed-race) nursemaid called Wilhelmina and had seven children by her and his second wife. The eldest, William Arthur Rollock, migrated to Trinidad and worked for the Trinidad Government Railway, then became the overseer of the Woodbrook estate, which he is said to have laid out when it became a suburb of Port of Spain early in the twentieth century. He was Beryl McBurnie's grandfather, and, she said, her first music teacher, from whom she learned about classical music and harmony.[5]

The Roberts Street house was originally the Woodbrook estate overseer's house. It had four bedrooms and an outside bathroom, and was eventually occupied by several of Rollock's eight children with his second wife (he had fifteen children in all). These were Wilhelmina McBurnie, the eldest, and four of her children; Alice, a housebound invalid; Clara; and Roy Ralph Rollock and three of his ten children (Roy, Denise and Vanetta).

Some of this generation of children attended the private

primary school Wilhelmina ran from home; she also gave sewing lessons. Her grandson Michael Germain remembers her as being very knowledgeable, and having a beautiful singing voice (she was a soprano, says his cousin Vanetta): she performed in concerts at the Prince's Building. Roy led a band, and both Wilhelmina's daughters had talents for music and dancing, as did some of her grandchildren and great-grandchildren (among them, Germain is a bassist, and his siblings have a family choir; Roy's daughter Denise danced with their cousin Beryl).

Beryl Eugenia McBurnie was the eldest of the four children of Wilhelmina and her husband, the mysterious William McBurnie (a rare surname in Trinidad, so he may have come from another island). Wilhelmina's niece Vanetta, despite growing up in the Rollock house with her two siblings, said they never met Mr McBurnie, their uncle: "It was said that he migrated to the States when the children were very young and never returned." Germain thinks Beryl's father lived in the Rollock house, but travelled a lot.

Beryl's sister Frieda, two years younger, was quieter and less eccentric, though she too could be exuberant, and was game for anything. She also studied in New York, danced with Beryl, and played music. She married an American businessman and had a son, David Artmann, but the marriage failed and Frieda returned home, where she taught art at a Woodbrook secondary school. She was well liked and admired, but seems to have been overshadowed by her elder sister's larger-than-life personality. They had two younger brothers: Arthur (born in 1916), who may have been a seaman and who migrated to the United States, and Roy (born in 1919), who is said to have had bipolar disorder, and lived with his mother until his death.

Michael Germain (chairman of the Little Carib Theatre's board since 2008) is the son of Wilhelmina's fifth child, Gladys Fraser. Gladys was a half-sister to Beryl and the other McBurnie children: her father was not Wilhelmina's husband, but Kenneth Fraser, a violinist in Wilhelmina's brother Roy's band. Wilhelmina may have taken up with Fraser after her husband died or left the family. Gladys was brought up with her father's family, elsewhere in Woodbrook.

Beryl was born on 2 November 1913, according to her birth certificate. The programme from her funeral says she was born in 1912; other sources, even close friends of hers, give dates ranging from 1907 to 1917. McBurnie never included her date of birth in documents such as her curriculum vitae. It is typical of her that it is hard to pin down even the year she was born; whether telling the story of her life, or building a theatre in her mother's back yard without planning permission, normal rules did not seem to apply to Beryl McBurnie.

The house where the McBurnies and the Rollocks lived has been described as a tiny wooden gingerbread house; Vanetta Rollock calls it "very modest". But the family was middle class, even though the house was among the smaller ones in the genteel district of Woodbrook. In addition, they would have considered themselves and been considered not black but coloured, an important class distinction in those days and in preceding generations; and one which would have helped give McBurnie the self-confidence that later allowed her to make outrageous demands in the furtherance of her cause. But although her optimism and persistence were all her own, her ideas were shared by many.

The little city of Port of Spain had been expanding for a century. Woodbrook, to the west, was bought by the Siegert family, manufacturers of Angostura bitters, in 1899, but in 1911 they sold it to the government. The old town of Port of Spain was still the commercial and administrative centre, but much of the city's housing had become run-down. Where once free African communities had flourished in the hills of Laventille and on the banks of the Dry River below, now those narrow streets harboured tiny shacks and the notorious barrack yards where entire families were crammed into one room each. Belmont, formerly known as Freetown, had also housed African communities, but the cottages packed along its alleys could not accommodate the numbers or the ambitions of the growing black and coloured middle class.

So they poured into the new houses along the wide, flat streets of Woodbrook, laid out in neat grids around grassy public squares, served by modern electric tramcars and lit by electric lights. C.L.R. James describes this lifestyle when Haynes, the protagonist of his 1936 novel *Minty Alley*, first looks through the front window of Mrs Rouse's lodging-house as he goes to rent a room there: "Through the open jalousies he could see a neat little drawing-room, centre-table, bent-wood chairs, antimacassars, what-nots and china ornaments."[6]

The McBurnie/Rollock family would have worshipped at the Tranquillity Methodist Church on Tragarete Road, completed in 1906. Their daughters were sent to Tranquillity Girls' School, around the corner from the church, once they had outgrown first Wilhelmina's school and then the (Presbyterian) Woodbrook Canadian Mission School (also known as Akal's, after its first principal), where their aunt Clara taught.

By then, Beryl, with her backyard concerts, was already showing the artistic talents and entrepreneurial spirit that shaped her life and many others. Whatever songs and dances she and the other little girls performed, they would have been European ones. Middle-class families sent their daughters to the ballet classes taught by Marie Palmer-Chizzola and other ladies, as well as to music lessons.

As for what was taught in schools at that time, James, a few years older than McBurnie, described his colonial education at Queen's Royal College in his autobiographical *Beyond a Boundary* (1963). Though the school was a very good one, he wrote, "it would have been more suitable to Portsmouth than to Port of Spain. . . . I learnt and obeyed and taught . . . the English public-school code." This was true of all government schools. In addition, colonial schools inculcated "the limitation on spirit, vision and self-respect which was imposed on us by the fact that our masters, our curriculum, our code of morals, *everything* began from the basis that Britain was the source of all light and leading, and our business was to admire, wonder, imitate, learn".[7]

Eric Williams, who led Trinidad and Tobago to independence and who was a staunch supporter of the Little Carib and what it symbolized, similarly described his own education at Tranquillity in his autobiography. To say it was British, he concluded, "is only another way of saying that it was un-West Indian. My training was divorced from anything remotely suggestive of Trinidad and the West Indies. . . . My arithmetical problems dealt with pounds, shillings, and pence in the classroom, but I had to reckon in dollars and cents when I went shopping for my mother."[8] McBurnie would have received a similar education at Tranquillity Girls' Intermediate, one of the first schools to begin preparing girls to sit the Cambridge secondary exams taken by boys.

In Williams's last year at Tranquillity Boys', one Captain J.O. Cutteridge was appointed principal. "His policy," wrote Williams, "was openly designed to make the school more English in its outlook." Within seven years of his arrival in Trinidad, Cutteridge's influence on the local curriculum was vastly increased when he became director of education. It was in this capacity that he published the textbooks for which he is now notorious. They were, wrote Williams, "One of the greatest innovations in the history of Trinidad. He published textbooks called West Indian Readers and West Indian Geographies. The idea was, pedagogically, irreproachable. But West Indian public opinion, and not only in Trinidad, considered that the books presented West Indian life in a disparaging light." Cutteridge was succeeded both at Tranquillity Boys' and in the education department by Captain E.W. Daniel, under whom McBurnie later worked (and whom she continued to admire; he was in turn a supporter of her theatre). Daniel also published textbooks, Williams wrote, "this time on West Indian history; these texts, admirable though they are as accounts of the annexation of the West Indies by various European powers, are everything or anything but West Indian histories".[9] What Williams learned at school about colonies and slavery was their history under the Roman empire, he recorded; it was not until 1939 that any West Indian history was included in the curriculum.[10]

McBurnie came to share James's and Williams's views on the inappropriateness of this "local" education. She met Williams when he taught briefly at the Government Training College before he left Trinidad for Oxford in 1932, then went to lecture at Howard University in 1939. Williams had replaced C.L.R. James at the college when the latter migrated to England in 1932; James then moved to the United States in 1938, the year McBurnie went to New York to study. His pamphlet *The Case for West Indian Self-Government* was published in Britain in 1933, and by then other Trinidadians too had raised that prospect, including the Beacon literary group, with which James had been associated. The trade unionist, writer and politician Albert Gomes, who ran the *Beacon* magazine, wrote in it in July 1931:

> Black man, bearded old son of a slave, your children are being slain by the dozens in America, in Africa, in the Indies. . . . Bare your fangs as the white man does. Cast off your docility. . . . You have to be savage like a white man to escape the white man's savagery. . . . Black man, you know. . . . You must know that the white man who pats you on the back and tells you how wonderful you are, is the white to be feared. . . . Run away from him, black man. He is your enemy, your bitter enemy.[11]

Gomes's contemporaries and collaborators on the *Beacon* and *Trinidad* magazine were also beginning to reflect on – and chafe against – the colony's rigidly stratified society and working-class experience in the cramped spaces of the barrack yards, in books such as James's *Minty Alley* and Alfred Mendes's *Pitch Lake* (1934) and *Black Fauns* (1935).

McBurnie would have been exposed to increasingly common anti-colonial views from these and other sources. In *Glory Dead* (1939), the left-wing English writer Arthur Calder-Marshall, after a visit to Trinidad, wrote:

> The role that Great Britain has played in foreign politics during the last three years has finally obliterated any belief in the old slogan that the British Empire has a sense of justice or feeling for the oppressed. . . . "This empire," says the West Indian, "is not our Empire. We don't want to have anything to do with it. At home it oppresses us. It resists all our attempts to get a straight deal as seditious. It jails our leaders, shadows our representatives with detectives, admits our grievances and then does nothing about them."[12]

The reference to Britain's foreign policies reflects the outrage felt by West Indians of African descent at the western democracies' failure to intervene after Italy invaded Ethiopia in 1935. Marcus Garvey had founded the Universal Negro Improvement Association in Jamaica in 1914, and his black nationalist call had been heard in Trinidad, where his *Negro World* publication was imported at least until it was deemed seditious by the authorities,[13] and his admiration for Ethiopia and its independence was shared.

These were tumultuous times in Trinidad and the region. Volunteers returning from World War I had been frustrated by discrimination against them in the British armed forces and the lack of decently paid employment on their homecoming; this led to the beginnings of the trade-union movement. Major labour unrest began in 1934. Although oil had been discovered in south Trinidad early in the century and was becoming increasingly important to the economy, there was still widespread, desperate poverty. An oilfield strike in 1937 spread to other areas, and moves to quell it led to fatalities and injuries. In 1938, the British government sent the Moyne Commission to the West Indies; although it was partly intended to assure the population of the colonial power's concern, its findings were so shocking that some were suppressed until 1945. Calder-Marshall reported a speech by Trinidad's governor, Sir Murchison Fletcher, who was sympathetic to the population and the striking workers, and whose superiors in London consequently forced him to resign. Calder-Marshall quotes Fletcher as saying: "When I arrived in Trinidad I was somewhat painfully struck by the poverty here", and citing a medical officer's report on the appalling malnutrition among the Indian sector of the population. (Indians had been brought to Trinidad as indentured labourers from 1845 to 1917 to replace the emancipated former slaves in the cane fields.) Calder-Marshall also wrote: "Though Great Britain has ruled the island for over a hundred and forty years, educational facilities are scandalously backward. Compulsory education exists only in San Fernando and Port of Spain, and the all-over percentage of illiteracy is 43.1 per cent."[14]

McBurnie would still have been at school during some of
these events. Of her education at Tranquillity, she said only
that she had a teacher "who was very interested in the dances
of Britain: the Highland Fling, the hornpipe and so on. I saw
the irony of that" ("Lady of the Big Idea", *Sunday Express*, 17
October 1993). In her early years, amateur musical and
dramatic groups would have staged shows and organized
performances by visiting professionals at the Prince's Building,
the Royal Victoria Institute in uptown Port of Spain and one
or two other venues. The Society of Independents, a contro-
versial group of visual artists, was formed in the 1930s, but
in theatre the pioneering Whitehall Players did not come
into being until 1946.[15]

Still, when the young McBurnie began learning about the
dance and music that made up part of the island's and the
region's cultural heritage, she was not the only Trinidadian
interested in researching the island's or the Caribbean's traditions. Steelband scholar Shannon Dudley points out, "As
early as the 1930s, middle-class intellectuals in Trinidad made
concerted efforts to document and promote local folklore."[16]
Thus it was that in 1933 or thereabouts, said McBurnie, she
bumped into the leading folklorist Andrew Carr under a
streetlight at the corner of Belmont Circular and Belle Eau
Road. She had known Carr for a long time: she claimed to
have approached him about a dance at a keep-fit club she
attended, aged eight, asking him to help in "shaping our feet
and our legs in an arc that would really make a beautiful
line". When she ran into Carr years later, he arranged for her
to meet his mother, who knew a lot about the Rada commu-

nity of Belmont Valley Road.[17] That was a turning point in McBurnie's life, she said: "my beginning in the research into the performing arts and . . . for the Little Carib".[18]

McBurnie started going on field trips with Carr, and possibly others who were interested in folk-dance retentions, Afro-Caribbean religion and other forms of creole folk culture, often a syncretism of African and European elements (as well as, to some extent, the Indian practices that survived in purer forms). They did not need to travel far. Albert Gomes wrote:

> Beneath the fragile crust, which the tourist or casual visitor to Trinidad observes, lies a totally different world anchored in the animism of earlier history. Drive five miles south of Port of Spain, with its clotted motor traffic and modern buildings, in any direction, to the hills of Diego Martin or Laventille or Maraval, and you have stepped out of one age into another. In this sense illuminated Port of Spain is an illusion. Its projection of metropolitan sophistication effectively camouflages the essential Trinidad, which is a rural reality belonging to the hills, valleys and gorges, the rivers and streams, the cane fields and cocoa plantations.[19]

Molly Ahye, later a principal dancer with the Little Carib Company, wrote that McBurnie already had a dance group of her own by this time, although it "maintained a low profile because of the cultural climate which was not prepared to accept as 'respectable' any attempts at performing what was [sic] considered 'slave' activities" (CCD, 3). In some quarters, given the anti-colonial mood among local intellectuals, by now this attitude was being challenged. Gomes commented on the mixed attitudes of Trinidadians towards their own history and culture: "It was the illiterate and semi-illiterate Negroes who kept the ancestral fires burning: who remained active in the Shouters during the difficult years of proscription; who continued to worship the dark gods of the Shango in the face of middle-class indifference and contempt; who filled the calypso tent with song and music . . . who invented the steelband and fought and died to keep it alive." When he defended these cultural forms, he went on, "how often did I hear from middle-class Negroes the criticism: Gomes wants to take the people back to their primitive past!" He noted the irony of his being a man of Portuguese descent "defending the rights of black West Indians to their racial heritage and being accused by black people like themselves of encouraging a discreditable retrogression". But in time he was vindicated: "It is to the Shouters and the Shango and the steelband and the calypso that all Trinidadians have turned, in their desperate search for a cultural individuality to match political independence. For these are all that they have and it is right therefore that they should cherish them."[20]

McBurnie felt as passionately as Gomes about the country's cultural heritage. The rise of nationalist, anti-colonial feeling and the investigation of traditional indigenous cultural forms fed into each other, and so it was that many of Trinidad's early political activists were frequently in the audience at the Little Carib. Nevertheless, McBurnie's decision to focus on dance might have seemed somewhat frivolous, given the political and social upheavals of the time. But dance played a special part in Caribbean and perhaps especially in Trinidad and Tobago's culture; in exploring it, McBurnie was not only casting off a colonial mindset but also reclaiming a far older artistic heritage.

When Columbus arrived in 1498, Trinidad had been inhabited for thousands of years by the First Peoples, who were labelled Caribs and Arawaks by the Spanish colonists, and mythologized respectively as belligerent cannibals and a peace-loving, lazy people who spent their time swinging in their hammocks. The Spanish tried to force these Amerindians to work for them, with little success. Some were worked or beaten to death. Some fell victim to European diseases to which they had no immunity. A few slipped away along ancient trails to the south coast, and then to the forests of South America, a few miles away.

The Spanish did little to exploit Trinidad. The British captured it in 1797, but even fifteen years later only 10 per cent of it was under cultivation. This was largely thanks to an earlier influx, in the 1780s, of planters from Grenada and Martinique: alarmed by the unrest in France, they sought a safer place to settle, bringing enslaved Africans with them, and the Spanish gave them grants of land to cultivate. Until then, the entire population had been fewer than three thousand.[21]

Even under the British, Trinidad never became a fully developed sugar colony, in contrast with islands like Jamaica, Barbados and Tobago; by the time Britain captured Trinidad, these islands had been under sugar for close to two hundred years, and had their own semi-autonomous governments. Trinidad instead became the first crown colony, ruled directly from Britain via the governor. It was not very British, though:

the population, enslaved and free, spoke a French patois, along with some Spanish, and it was only in the 1840s that Governor Lord Harris began a drive to anglicize both the language and the laws. Nevertheless, many people spoke patois up until the 1940s, and French and Spanish cultural influences also lingered.

Ten years after Trinidad became a British colony, the slave trade was abolished in the British empire, sealing the fate of the sugar economies of the West Indies, and especially Trinidad, which had always had a labour shortage. The Royal Navy captured slave ships passing through the Caribbean en route to Cuba and Brazil, and some of the recently enslaved Africans on board were freed and deposited in Trinidad, where it was hoped they would supply the needed workforce. Instead, many formed free communities in east Port of Spain; they worked in the city as tradesmen and businessmen, but retained many of their own practices and beliefs.

Meanwhile, before emancipation in 1834, enslaved workers on the estates spent much of the free time allowed them – Saturday evening to Monday morning – holding dances: this was one of the few occasions when they were allowed to gather and to spend their time as they pleased. The planters imposed restrictions on the dances, such as limiting the hours when it was permitted to beat African drums; they feared these gatherings might turn to insurrections, especially after the success of the Haitian revolution in 1804. But for the enslaved labourers, the weekend dances were, among other things, a chance to forget the misery of their lives and lose themselves in the music. They combined elements of each other's traditional dances, as well as European dances they found appealing. This was a particularly rich mixture in Trinidad, whose European-descended inhabitants came from so many countries and many of whose African-descended people had never been enslaved, or only briefly.[22]

These were the dances that McBurnie learned on her nocturnal expeditions with Carr or her dancers into the countryside or some of the less middle-class, Europeanized areas of Port of Spain. Her area of interest was novel, but in setting out to discover more about the African origins of local culture, of which some Trinidadians were beginning to be conscious and even proud, McBurnie was part of a movement. Her research trips were remarkable, however, because of her class and gender; few respectable middle-class girls would have dared to undertake such expeditions. What her family thought of these ventures has not been recorded. They probably disapproved, but thanks to her charm, self-confidence and determination, Beryl was never a person to whom anyone could easily say no.

McBurnie used these qualities to get what she wanted – a useful ability in later years when she had to raise money or find anything else the Little Carib Theatre needed. "Every word she speaks in her nervous, tender voice", wrote American reporter Betty Reef ("West Indians Gain Respect for Heritage by Dancing", *Amarillo Globe-Times*, 20 October 1961, 15), obviously fascinated by McBurnie, "is accompanied by 'body English'. Her bright eyes flash and roll, her expressive hands [wave], her feet tap". "Nervous" here does not mean timid; rather, McBurnie was highly strung and bursting with ideas. She had a racing mind, and her conversation jumped from one topic to another; but, said Ron Julien, one of her dancers, "She was bright enough to do anything she wanted."

She always dressed the part, too, ensuring she looked striking, if not downright eccentric; many of those who knew her commented on her outfits. Anne Sandfort, who danced for McBurnie in the latter's last years, remembered:

> Beryl always wore a black, long-sleeved leotard and a long dance skirt. The skirt was sometimes a colourful one but she mostly wore black. She always had a head tie . . . She loved big (gaudy) jewellery. Big colourful beads around her neck and bracelets. . . . She liked pearls too. She was heavy on the feet and you heard Beryl coming and her bracelets clanging. She liked to stop and poise her neck mid-walk. She was simply impressive and eccentric.[23]

These costumes were an important outward expression of McBurnie's independent spirit and forcefulness. She liked to stand out, in all sorts of ways.

All these elements, plus her knowledge of local folk-dance traditions, her recognition of their importance and her sense of possessing a mission, no doubt played a large part in her decision to return to Trinidad after studying and performing abroad.

TWO

You can still see Beryl McBurnie dancing, thanks to two surviving scraps of film footage from her glory days in New York in the 1940s. Under her stage name of Belle Rosette, she is decorous in the full-scale, long-sleeved Martiniquan *douillette* folk costume, complete with headtie. To two calypsoes, McBurnie dances energetically but demurely, with lots of arm movement, swinging her hips just a little, gathering up handfuls of her madras skirt to flash voluminous petticoats below, but showing no more than an ankle. In the second one, as Sam Manning sings, "Willie, Willie, don't go from me", McBurnie twirls and smiles, steps back and forth and works her arms. Sometimes she withdraws a little and her two backing dancers come forward in more flirtatious mode.

These "soundies" illustrate perfectly McBurnie's dancers' later comments on her style: she never wined, and she disapproved of her dancers doing so. Her dancing was proper, and no doubt based on traditional steps, with no suggestive or erotically inclined moves. In the films, she dances with tremendous confidence and an unfaltering, genuine-looking smile, and certainly possesses charisma: she is the dancer to whom one's eyes are drawn, whatever the other two are doing, though her performance is simple, brisk and certainly not technically spectacular. Nor does she make the slightest attempt to portray a seductive "island girl".

These films, the only visual record of her professional work in New York, are the equivalent of the music videos of today. "Soundies" were short films made not with voiceovers or music tracks overlaid on a silent film, but with actual soundtracks. These are also the only known calypso soundies – calypso was in vogue in New York – and both date from 1943, two years before McBurnie returned home. Although not the headline act, she received credits at the start of both, which gives some indication of her status.[24] As "Belle Rosette" ("Beautiful Little Rose"), McBurnie was, for a time, one of the most popular black dancers in New York City's cabaret and theatre scene.

The soundies, *Quarry Road* and *Willie Willie*, by LOL Productions Incorporated, both feature Manning, a Trinidadian who became well known as a calypsonian after moving to New York in the early 1920s. Belle Rosette's name appears beneath his, but she shares the spotlight with him. The scene is a staged, cramped nightclub setting, with a few smiling black and white patrons. A small band of guitars and brass instruments backs Manning, who moves around the set singing lyrics about "Bajan gal don't wash she clothes till the rain come down", before the song segues into a medley. An energetic bare-chested man in flared, slit tiger-skin pants leaps into the foreground and dances briefly, then is replaced by Rosette and two other light-skinned female dancers. The others (one is McBurnie's sister Frieda) are more scantily clad, with crop tops that bare their stomachs. *Willie Willie* was filmed on the same set in the same costumes, presumably on the same occasion.

Perhaps McBurnie's performance in these soundies was deliberately relatively low-key in order to complement rather than distract from Manning, the headline act. Her dancing in them is not original or exciting enough to account for the reputation she had gained in New York. Her use of a stage name also perhaps betrays that some stigma was still attached to the idea of a woman pursuing a stage career – at least in Trinidad, if perhaps less so by then in New York. That name might have sounded merely exotic and picturesque to her American audiences. But that she used a French-patois pseudonym, Gérard Besson points out, shows her attachment to her Afro-creole roots – the wellspring of her work as a dancer and choreographer.[25]

McBurnie had left Trinidad for the United States in 1938. There are varying accounts – from McBurnie herself – of how she came to study dance in New York, and for how long. In 1941, in an interview with American journalist Marvel Cooke, "in the tiny studio apartment she makes her own over on east 102nd" (in East Harlem), McBurnie said her father had been "her mentor, encouraging her in her ambition"; a few years before, he had taken her "on a trip through the islands . . . studying native songs and dances". He had sent her to New York twice, "to study dramatics (her first

love . . .) and dancing at the Academy of Allied Arts".
McBurnie added, "But he died a short time ago and I've been
on my own ever since."

Likewise, Molly Ahye quotes McBurnie as writing that the
plan had always been for her to study dance in the United
States, to further her dream "to build a theatre in her mother's
backyard" (*CCD*, 3).[26] But in a 1993 interview, McBurnie said
that when she left Trinidad, her family did not want her to
be a dancer: they thought it was a "terrible, terrible idea" –
though it may have been *her* plan all along. "My father took
me to America to become a doctor," she said then, adding
revealingly, "but I don't have the organisation, the discipline
. . . that would be a straitjacket." On the voyage, in this
account, the ship's captain took young Beryl's side and persuaded her father to let her study acting rather than medicine. But as it turned out, Beryl did not need the captain's
help, since, she said, her father died five days after they
landed. In any case, she added casually: "I must do exactly as
I want to do" ("Lady of the Big Idea", *Sunday Express*, 17 October 1993). The comment illustrates her famously indomitable
will, the determination which was her greatest strength and
which also got her into trouble, when her single-mindedness
made her seem eccentric or led her to insist on her own way
against other people's better judgement.

In another version, she went to New York in 1938 because
her father had fallen ill there (he may have been living there
all along). He wanted her to study medicine, then get married,
like other girls; but he died five days later. McBurnie returned
to Trinidad,[27] where she taught during the day, ran a dance

school in the afternoons and "with her sister, also a dancer, gave concerts from time to time". From all these jobs she "scraped and saved until she had enough to return to America last fall to study the dance with Martha Graham at Columbia".[28]

If McBurnie's father really had left the family years before, perhaps some of these conflicting stories – in which he is the ideal, concerned patriarch, offering support and guidance – represent the wishful thinking of a girl who grew up in a crowded and financially precarious household, peopled mainly by women and other children, her younger siblings and cousins.

McBurnie was vague about what exactly she studied in the United States, for how long and with whom. Perhaps the most reliable guide is a 1949 job application she sent to Sydney Hogben, Trinidad's director of education, which showed she did not graduate from Columbia, as is sometimes thought, and studied under Martha Graham for only one semester. McBurnie wrote to Hogben that at Columbia Teachers College, she had taken summer sessions in 1938 in rhythms for children, play production, and painting and drawing; in autumn and winter 1940 she did Dalcroze eurhythmics and dance composition and modern technique, the latter two under Graham. She did only one more semester at Columbia, in 1945, when she studied voice and diction, accompaniment for dance and stagecraft. In 1938, she studied modern dance technique under Charles Weidman at the Academy of Allied Art, and in the fall and winter of that year did black-and-white art and watercolour at the Works Project Administration. Between 1940 and 1945 she dropped her studies to focus on performing, but in the latter year, as well as her three summer courses at Columbia, she had private tuition in Shakespeare from Abbie Mitchell. Ahye also records that McBurnie studied eurhythmics with Elsa Findlay, gave lecture demonstrations at the Henry Street Settlement Playhouse, and taught West Indian dance at the prestigious New Dance Group Studio in 1944 (*CCD*, 3).[29] A clipping from the *New York Amsterdam News* (28 October 1944, 11B) says she taught "the dramatic dance, posture and body building exercises and dances of the West Indies" at the Mura Dehn Academy of Swing, with no mention of the New Dance Group. It is possible she taught at both; but the *New York Age* (20 October 1945, 4) reported that Belle Rosette "was presented" in a lecture demonstration by the New Dance Group, with no reference to her being on the faculty there.

Ahye also says that in New York, McBurnie "became very active in teaching the music and dances of the West Indies and in particular, those of Trinidad and Tobago" (*CCD*, 3). Though certainly she had studied local dance, it is not clear how McBurnie would have learned the dances of other countries by this point; perhaps on the trip with her father that she described to Marvel Cooke in 1941. McBurnie also told Ahye she gave the prominent African American dancer Katherine Dunham private lessons in kalinda and bongo, and taught her Shango (Orisha) chants. But Dunham's biographer Ruth Beckford, one of Dunham's dancers, does not mention McBurnie's name. She refers to Dunham's visit to Trinidad during her 1935 Caribbean research trip in passing – and

Dunham set a 1940s musical, *Carib Song*, in Trinidad; but
Dunham's main interest in the Caribbean was Haiti.[30]

McBurnie undoubtedly taught the noted dancer Pearl
Primus, who was born in Laventille, Trinidad, in 1919, but
moved with her family to New York at two. Primus did not
begin to study dance until around 1940, but she was a born
dancer. By late 1942, she was applying to present solo dance
performances at the cultural centre of the Young Men's
Hebrew Association, known as the 92nd Street Y, on the
Upper East Side, listing among her teachers "Belle Rosette
as her instructor in 'Primitive' dance". The *Y Bulletin* said
Primus had "studied West Indian dance forms with Belle
Rosette, dancer and choreographer, and has appeared with
her in 'Antilliana' at the Museum of Modern Art, the 'Y'
Dance Theatre and the Baltimore Museum of Art".[31] Primus
became well known in her own right, but her biographers,
Peggy and Murray Schwartz, are generous in stressing that
other progressive dancers and choreographers were already
exploring their African heritage:

> Even before her leap onto the stage followed by her African
> journey, black dancers were beginning to form companies and
> break into the world of concert dance, resisting an attitude
> among some blacks as well as whites that their dances were
> shamefully "primitive". Eugene von Grona, a German refugee,
> brought the American Negro Ballet to the Lafayette Theatre in
> Harlem in 1937; the African dancer Asadata Dafora's African
> Dance Theater was performing in New York in the late 1930s;
> Katherine Dunham's first full-length ballet, "L'Ag 'Ya", was per-
> formed in 1938; Beryl McBurnie, performing as Belle Rosette

from Trinidad, performed *Antilliana* in 1941. Indeed, Pearl performed with McBurnie in 1942.

Primus herself always acknowledged this debt, telling an
interviewer in 1989: "I was influenced by Beryl McBurnie,
who is the cultural dance teacher and driving force from
Trinidad, so Trinidad is strongly in me."[32]

There is another, less straightforward link between Primus
and McBurnie. In 1941, McBurnie told Marvel Cooke she
had recently "created" a dance to Billie Holiday's "Strange
Fruit", the chilling song about lynchings. "That is a perfectly
marvelous song," McBurnie said, "and the rhythm and mood
certainly lend themselves to the dance." Her version was a
dance of skeletons, and she said it was "quite effective", leading
Cooke to gush about her candour and the way she "simply
states facts as they [are] – unadorned".[33] But although
McBurnie may have believed everything she said, many facts
about her time in New York are hard to ascertain, and the
story of "Strange Fruit" is among them. There are references
to her choreographing not only to folk music but also to classical music in Trinidad; but "Strange Fruit" is utterly different
from the other material she performed in the United States
– West Indian folk dance and cheery calypso. Meanwhile,
Pearl Primus's biographers write about a dance she performed
to readings of the original poem "Strange Fruit", or sometimes
without any accompaniment; they describe it as "a solo Pearl
created", danced in the persona of a white woman. It brought
audiences to their feet at her first solo performance at the
92nd Street Y in 1943, and the Schwartzes describe it as

depicting "pure anguish . . . pain that is bone-deep . . . the recognition of an irreversible human cruelty".[34] The dance seems more in keeping with Primus's oeuvre than McBurnie's, although it is possible that Primus worked on it under McBurnie's tutelage, or that the two women independently created entirely different versions.

What is clear is that as a dancer and singer, McBurnie soon attracted attention in New York. Marvel Cooke described her mesmerizing performance when she appeared as a supporting act to a Brazilian opera singer in 1941:

> The curtains parted to reveal Belle Rosette – a slender bronze girl in a flowing and colorful Chango [sic] costume – an infectious grin lighting her gamin face . . . She poised there on her toes for a split second and then, at the first beat of the drums . . . Belle Rosette executed the first sinuous and sensuous moves of the Chango, a dance she brought with her from her native Trinidad.
>
> Excitement was high. No longer was the audience nice and polite and remote. It completely lost its face and became rowdy in paying obeisance to this girl from Trinidad who completely stole the show from the star. When it quieted down after a third encore, she sang a Calypso song about the Germans surrendering to the British. She was no longer a dancer – but a minx kidding the life out of the Axis dictators. She waved a newspaper high in the air, crying: "Argos paper! Lates' telegram, Germans surrender under the British comman'!"[35]

McBurnie was soon prominently billed in shows at prestigious venues that included the Museum of Modern Art, the Brooklyn Academy of Music, the 92nd Street Y, and the Baltimore

Museum of Art, as well as appearing frequently at clubs and theatres such as the Village Vanguard and the Harlem Apollo.

She first became known outside Harlem in early 1941, thanks to a series of "Coffee Concerts" at the Museum of Modern Art arranged by Louise Crane, who read about her in a story by Cooke. Crane had begun producing these concerts, starring "young Negro artists", because, she told Cooke in an interview, "I just believe in ignoring prejudices . . . I am interested in good music" (*New York Amsterdam Star-News*, 28 June 1941, 20). After seeing McBurnie in a show starring the calypsonian Macbeth the Great, Crane signed her as a client and booked her for a Coffee Concert in May, *South American Panorama* (also glowingly reviewed by Cooke). McBurnie starred in another Coffee Concert on 10 November 1941 – *Antilliana*, which was reviewed by "H.D." (the poet Hilda Doolittle), who described Belle Rosette as "exuding a cabaret species of glamour" (*American Dancer*, January 1942, 15); it was in this show, revived in April 1942, that Pearl Primus first performed with her. Belle Rosette is mentioned often in reviews of such shows, described as a "calypso singer and dancer", and at least once as "perhaps the first female Calypso singer in the business". (The *New York Amsterdam Star-News* [19 July 1941, 20] was correct in describing her as a "calypso singer": in Trinidad the term "calypsonian" is generally reserved for those who both write and perform calypso. McBurnie sang and danced to popular calypsoes, but did not write them. She was by no means the first woman in Trinidad to sing calypso.)

Antilliana was staged again in 1943. Schwartz and Schwartz record:

> On January 8 and 9 Primus performed again in *Antilliana*, at the Baltimore Museum of Art. *Antilliana* addresses the history of the West Indies and the mix of cultures in the region from 1492 onward, including Spanish, French, English, and African. The program said, "The Shango, Voodoo, Plavoodoo, Rhada [sic], and Bongo are the best known among the African dances, and are practiced in the backwoods of the country, away from the cynical eye. They are danced to the accompaniment of drums and generally take the form of rituals, expressing long suffering and sacrifice. The Beguine, Belle Air [sic], Meringue [sic] and Rondo are popular among the French. In a lighter vein than the African, they are more on the order of country dances, expressing a delightful light-heartedness and gaiety. Spanish waltzes and the Bomba are best known among the Spaniards. The Calypso as an art form is an excellent example of the fusion of racial elements that is so typical of the West Indies."[36]

As well as Beryl McBurnie and Primus, the dancers included Frieda McBurnie, and the pianist was the leading Trinidadian musician Lionel Belasco.

A programme from the Brooklyn Academy of Music for a "Caribbean Program" on 13 December 1941 lists Belle Rosette as the headline act, along with the Haitian Rada Group. She performed "The Obeah Woman: Necromancy of the West Indies", then a "Burroquite Dance: from the Trinidad carnival of olden days", and "Shango: Voodoo ritual practiced by descendants of Africans in Trinidad". She appeared in "Street Scenes of Trinidad" with the Haitians, then sang "Calypso

News", performed "Woopsin: Modern Calypso Dance" with the Haitians, and sang "Ugly Woman". ("Woopsin" was a 1941 calypso by the Roaring Lion; his "Ugly Woman" dated from 1934.) Rosette also sang "Folk songs of the islands", several songs in patois from St Lucia, Martinique and Dominica, and did a Martiniquan dance. The grand finale was "Shouters from Sobo", described as "Singing and dancing of the Shouter sect of the village of Sobo".

On 18 April 1942, Bill Chase's "All Ears" showbiz column in the *New York Amsterdam Star-News* reported that after a recital at the 92nd Street Y, McBurnie had flown to Fisk University to perform, then back to New York to audition for the Paramount film company. In October, she appeared in another, "star-studded" Coffee Hour at the Harlem Defense Recreation Center, billed as a "famous Calypso singer and dancer, who took over Carmen Miranda's role in 'Sons O'Fun' for one night" (*New York Age*, 10 October 1942, 4). This latter was a major achievement, as Miranda was a huge star. Announcing this triumph, the *People's Voice* said that at a Coffee Concert Rosette had "completely won over her audience with a superb demonstration of showmanship", and prophesied, "A year from now she'll probably be one of Broadway's great stars. She's different, definitely different" (cited in *CCD*, 13). But McBurnie's path did not lie along Broadway.

While her New York career appeared to be going well, McBurnie returned to Trinidad several times during the war years, possibly to research and choreograph new work to stage in the United States, as well as to raise funds to continue her studies. In 1940, she organized the first performance by her Trinidad group, *A Trip through the Tropics,* on 6 August at the Empire Theatre, Port of Spain, under the patronage of Governor Sir Hubert Young and his wife. The *Port of Spain Gazette* called it an artistic success, and "one of the most interesting and artistic recitals ever staged in Trinidad. Crowds were forced to return home due to the limited space in the theatre, and with one voice the public is clamouring for a repeat" (cited in *CCD,* 5). *A Trip through the Tropics,* repeated at the Prince's Building on 15 August, incorporated some pieces from *Antilliana.* It included McBurnie's "Obeah Woman", "Shouters from Sobo", "Bongo" and "Shango"; the calypsoes "Money Is King" and "Ugly Woman"; and folk songs sung by her and the cast, as well as pieces danced by others. It was billed in the programme as being presented by "Beryl McBurnie and Group".

McBurnie also returned home in 1942 and 1944, despite the dangers to shipping from German ships and submarines. The entertainment scene in Trinidad was booming: potential audiences now included thousands of American servicemen stationed on the island, since as well as being a source of petroleum, Trinidad was important to the United States as a defence against possible Nazi attacks via West Africa or from Vichy-controlled French Caribbean territories.

After her sojourns at home, McBurnie returned to the United States. But a tiny clipping in the *Chicago Defender* reported on 25 November 1944 that Belle Rosette, "the singer and dancer from Trinidad who created such a sensation here a few years ago", had returned home "to recuperate from a recurrent illness". There are no other references to this illness;

and the paper's description of her makes her sound as if McBurnie's star was fading in the United States. How far, one wonders, did that star really rise? In announcing that she was to substitute for Carmen Miranda, a story whose headline called McBurnie a "Harlem Girl" declared the occasion "one of the few times in recent memory that a relatively unknown performer has replaced a big name" (*New York Amsterdam Star-News*, 4 April 1942, 16). Her audition for Paramount led to nothing; her one-night stand-in for Miranda was not repeated. Many of her stage appearances were in the Coffee Concerts, performed by black artists, and whose audiences may also have been primarily black. Others were at benefits for black organizations such as "A Tribute to Negro Servicemen", and shows for the National Association for the Advancement of Colored People, or the National Urban League, which aimed to "build a more secure place for Negro citizens in American democracy" (*New York Amsterdam Star-News*, 23 January 1943, 10). Meanwhile, at mainstream dance venues, Rosette was considered a novelty, and what white audiences expected was not something she was willing to deliver.

The fate of Carmen Miranda is instructive. Born in Brazil in 1909, Miranda was a samba dancer, singer and actress. She appeared on Broadway, then in a Hollywood film; but although in 1945 she was the highest-paid woman in the United States, there she was always regarded as exotic because of her accent and flamboyant costumes. Meanwhile, in Brazil and elsewhere in Latin America she was criticized for playing a clichéd Latina coquette. By the end of the war, American film audiences were losing interest in her, although her stage career continued. She suffered from depression partly brought on by her compatriots' reaction, and died of a heart attack at forty-six.

McBurnie was explicitly likened to Miranda in a review of her 1942 performance at Fisk University (a historically black university in Tennessee) by one Alvin S. Wiggers, who called her "a Miranda in miniature, with the same rapid gestures and movements, the rapid patter of words, and quick changing facial expressions. She wore a succession of colorful dresses, with gaudy bandanna headdress or bunch of plumes . . . she was barefooted and instead of Portuguese her language was a sort of French and English mixture." Wiggers described her accompaniment, by musicians including the highly regarded Haitian drummer Alphonse Cimber, as "weird drum effects from strange instruments" (*Tennessean*, 14 April 1942, 9).

McBurnie could not have been pleased by uninformed, patronizing and racist commentary of this sort; and there was a lot of it. Even a black paper, the *Baltimore Afro-American* (25 April 1942, 15) called her a "Tribal Dancer" in announcing that she would replace Miranda on Broadway. The *New York Amsterdam News* (15 November 1941, 15) said her "Blue Devil" demonstrated "the voodoo frenzy of the African dances". Bill Chase of the "All Ears" column wrote condescendingly that her replacing Miranda was "a bit of o.k. for anyone, especially if you're on the sepia side and comparatively unknown" (*New York Amsterdam News*, 18 April 1942, 8). Even her admirer Marvel Cooke said she was "no longer a girl from the hills of

Trinidad dancing her heart out at dusk to forget the hardships of the day".[37]

McBurnie may have come to believe that for American audiences, like Miranda's accent and artificial-fruit-topped headgear, the popularity of her work was a fad unlikely to last – and by the time she returned home she was already in her thirties. As a performer, her success may have been hampered by her middle-class ideas of propriety and her Methodist upbringing, since, being black and West Indian, she was expected to be seductive. A reviewer in the *Norfolk New Journal and Guide* (25 April 1942, 15) called her version of the calypso "Bay Street Gals" "one of her saucy numbers, but I think even the Bay Street Gals would object to the amount of refinement which she gave it". Although McBurnie enjoyed performing, she was anything but a showgirl. But it was difficult to break out of the stereotype Americans wanted her to fit, and at least as hard to prove herself as a serious artist. McBurnie's dances were grounded in research, but although she gave some lecture demonstrations, these demonstrations seem to have been mostly extemporized; she lacked the mental discipline and training for more formal study and teaching, though she did some of the latter. She was not a ballet dancer or an academic, like Graham, Dunham or Primus; her main interests were folk dance and song.

Meanwhile, friends and supporters (including Eric Williams) urged her to return home. Shannon Dudley comments: "McBurnie was undoubtedly under pressure from Trinidadian friends and colleagues to resist the pull of the commercial entertainment world. Critics in Trinidad heralded

McBurnie's success abroad, but their nationalist pride made them all the more concerned that McBurnie's work be perceived as more than simple entertainment."[38]

McBurnie always said she wanted to return home eventually: she told Cooke in 1941 that her ambition was "to return to Trinidad some day to establish a school of the dance".[39] Other factors as well as the difficulty of breaking into the mainstream may have influenced that decision. Gérard Besson points out that McBurnie's fair skin, which afforded her relatively privileged treatment in the "shadist" West Indies, meant nothing in the United States, where you were either black or white, and where segregation was still practised. Much of the way she was treated there must have seemed hostile and demeaning to her.

There were signs, too, that perhaps it was time to return home. The *New York Amsterdam News* (1 May 1943, 14), reporting on the first nightclub performance by McBurnie's protégée Pearl Primus, called her a "startling young dancer"; that she was part of McBurnie's company was mentioned as an afterthought. Paul Robeson went backstage to congratulate her. The paper reported that Primus, twenty-three, had originally wanted to be a doctor, but was now studying under Charles Weidman and Martha Graham (a story oddly similar to McBurnie's later account of her own beginnings in New York). Another notice highlighted the "sensational" Primus in McBurnie's *Tropics*. Audiences found Primus "charming"; entertainment columnist Bill Chase enthused, "she's got everything that makes for a true artist" (*New York Amsterdam News*, 1 May 1943, 8). Was Primus, less restrained and far

more athletic than McBurnie, replacing her as the leading
black dancer of the day? Primus grew up in New York, and
may have found it easier to be considered a bona fide dancer,
not merely a colourful outsider. More academically inclined
than McBurnie, she acquired a doctorate in anthropology.
Primus's biographers also quote Marjorie Boothman, sister
of Boscoe and Geoffrey Holder, who thought McBurnie "an
ambitious woman who found New York too big a place to
master".[40]

After recuperating from her mystery illness in Trinidad,
McBurnie returned to New York one last time, in October
1945, when she "was presented" at the New Dance Group,
and gave "a major lecture demonstration on Caribbean dance"
at Columbia University. The American researcher and lover
of Trinidad culture Ray Funk quotes the *Amsterdam News*
reviewer as saying: "She made a shockingly beautiful picture.
. . . With West Indian rhythms at the focal point, she spoke
illustrating with movements and drums, the folk arts of the
island, giving examples of games, folk tales, proverbs, folk
songs and dances." Funk also says McBurnie was offered a
post at Columbia, but turned it down. Her last public performance in New York, he writes, was at the Caribbean Festival sponsored by the West Indies National Council, on Fifth
Avenue, on 9 December 1945. Funk argues that McBurnie
left "at the height of her popularity", citing Walter Winchell's
syndicated newspaper column "On Broadway", which
reported that month: "Agents are flocking to West Indian
Harlem to see Belle Rosette (Calypso dancer and thrush)."[41]

What opportunities were those agents offering? It is

difficult to imagine what direction McBurnie's career might have taken had she remained in the United States, so deeply was she rooted in Caribbean folk tradition. Albert Gomes wrote in the *Trinidad Guardian* that year:

> She is possessed of vast resources of imagination which she employs to interpret in bold and colourful patterns the elan of her island home. Her forms are emboldened by a dramatic fervour that succeeds admirably in reproducing the basic primitive character of their inspiration. . . . It is Africa that is her inspiration; and the immediate fount from which she draws is the tradition of song and dance that persists tenaciously in Trinidad. (Quoted in *CCD*, 18)

It was perhaps inevitable that McBurnie turned her face against possible stardom, packed her bags and sailed for home.

THREE

One evening in early 1958, Hugh Bonterre heard the unexpected sound of African drumming coming from a back yard in Woodbrook. He had just got out of a taxi on Tragarete Road, and was heading for his family's new home on White Street, when he heard the music from behind a house on the corner of Roberts Street. The view from the pavement was hidden by a coconut-palm-leaf fence, so he pushed the dry fronds aside to see what was going on.

On the other side of the fence, Beryl McBurnie's sharp ears heard the rustling. She stopped the drumming and looked to see who was peeping in. Spotting young Bonterre, she ordered him, "Come here!" In those days young people did what an adult commanded, and Bonterre stepped into the Little Carib – then still only the back yard of 95 Roberts Street.

"Take off your shoes and go on the floor," McBurnie commanded. And that was how Bonterre auditioned for the Little Carib Dance Company. Still in awe of McBurnie – like all his peers – he describes this baptism of fire almost sixty years ago as "destiny". He had been involved in dance and drama before; it was part of his mixed French and Spanish heritage. His talent meant that though he only joined the company in January, he was selected to go on tour in July. He became known as "Shokolo", rechristened by McBurnie from the words to a Shango chant to which the company danced, because he had picked up the lyrics at once (young men whose names she did not immediately remember were all rechristened "Sonny boy").

Other youths were inveigled into joining the company in the same way: Ron Julien recalls one boy cycling past McBurnie's own home in St James – repurposed as the "Folk House" – who stopped to watch and was likewise ordered to show whether he could dance: McBurnie had picked up on his curiosity. Maureen Marquez-Sankeralli's son came to visit the theatre, and was told to take off his shirt, handed a shield and sent onstage as an Arawak.

Julien himself first danced under McBurnie's tutelage in 1955, when Princess Margaret came to Trinidad and McBurnie was commissioned to stage a gala show at the Queen's Park Oval. He was fifteen, and attended Tranquillity School (McBurnie was teaching physical education at the girls' school at the time). He had never danced before, and although afterwards he too sometimes peeped through the fence at events at the Little Carib, and played pan with Invaders, it was not until years later that he got fully involved with the theatre.

Maureen Marquez-Roebuck (later Marquez-Sankeralli) was first McBurnie's pupil at what was then Holy Faith Convent (now St Theresa's). One of four sisters, she came from a musical family and had already attended ballet classes and performed in school choirs and concerts. McBurnie officially taught physical education, but really taught dance: she would get the girls to improvise skits, for instance telling them to move as if they were *marchandes* (street vendors). She looked out for talent, and invited the best to join her junior company, the Humming Birds. By seventeen, Marquez-Roebuck was part of the senior company and toured Jamaica; she later became a principal dancer.

John "Buddy" Williams and his band provided music for the shows (and his wife was "the costume lady"; the Williamses lived nearby on Roberts Street). Orisha drummer Andrew Beddoe was an integral part of the Little Carib. Eric Williams would come to rehearsals and take notes, and McBurnie would consult him on the accuracy of her history.[42]

McBurnie's aunt or her mother Wilhelmina, known to the company as Aunty Willie, would cook for them during rehearsals; they would always be offered food – whether curry, pelau or just sandwiches, if there was nothing else – since they would rehearse all day when they were available. McBurnie's niece Vanetta Rollock Williams remembered, "On the nights of shows the dancers would all be in the house getting dressed, while Aunty Willie would be ironing costumes or sometimes even finishing making/adjusting them. The house would be buzzing with all kinds of people running in and out as Aunty Clara would be cooking meals for the dancers afterwards" (email to the author, 16 October 2017).

The dancers all worked; it was many years until they could be paid a stipend that covered even the cost of transport (Yvonne Sandy and other company members lived in

Belmont, and regularly walked miles from there and back for rehearsals). American photographer Earl Leaf, who turned to McBurnie for help in researching traditional local dance in 1948, wrote of the Little Carib dancers: "The members of her company proved to be as interesting as their dance repertoire. Stenographers, store clerks, college students, a nurse, school teacher, factory hands and office workers, they all had one thing in common, a love for the dance. Their interest and enthusiasm seemed boundless." He also recognized the outstanding talent of some members. "Among the dancers . . . I noticed several outstanding artists who could arouse welcome enthusiasm in a metropolitan concert hall: Irma Jarrett, Sheila Clark [later Boscoe Holder's wife], Jean Coggins, Geoffrey Holder, Ezme Brown, Percy Boarde [sic], Llewellyn Rock, Stanley Skeet and others."[43]

Aubrey Adams, later manager of the Little Carib and founder of his own dance company, recalled, many years later, some of the ordeals McBurnie put him through for the sake of their art: sometimes she would come to the government office where he was a clerk to make him rehearse for a show during his lunch hour. The other clerks watched him while McBurnie beat time on a desk. Similarly, Molly Ahye recalled, "I worked with BWIA [the national airline], I had children, but I'd rehearse till one in the morning. I danced while I was pregnant. Beryl could get you to do anything. You could be sick in bed and Beryl would come and say she was in trouble – and you would creep out of that bed and get well" ("Lady of the Big Idea", *Sunday Express*, 17 October 1993).

Nevertheless, that Hugh Bonterre was still peeping through a fence made of branches in 1958 showed McBurnie had not yet been able to charm up the funds needed to create the theatre she had envisaged. Pearl Connor (née Nunez) recalled that when she began dancing with McBurnie in 1940, "Teaching took place in open air, on the family patio, under the coconut trees" ("Beryl McBurnie", *Guardian* [UK], 29 April 2000). "It was like a big chicken coop," remembered Michael Smart, who would wait there while his mother, Vera (Luke) Smart, rehearsed (a friend of McBurnie, she danced with the company until 1951–52). "It had a dirt floor, chickens, a palm-leaf fence."[44] Adams remembered that its first roof was of galvanize (corrugated zinc).

While doing research in Cayenne (French Guiana) in 1945, McBurnie saw "a little intimate theatre", which she sketched as a model for her own ("Lady of the Big Idea", *Sunday Express*, 17 October 1993). The original Little Carib was behind the McBurnies' house, and opened onto White Street, to the east: Beryl had talked her mother and aunts into giving up their garden. She told an American reporter in 1961 that Hugh Wooding, then chairman of BWIA, had persuaded a group of businessmen to pay for the theatre's southern wall. "Beryl had already built the eastern wall for 903 painfully raised dollars. The stage, which is the western wall, was the first to be finished" ("West Indians Gain Respect", *Amarillo Globe-Times*, 20 October 1961, 15). The audience sat on folding chairs and on a balcony on the eastern (White Street) side. McBurnie's nephew Michael Germain, who helped put out the seats for performances, remembered the space was so tiny that a cast member once tumbled over the wall into the neighbours' chicken coop, and the show was accompanied by outraged squawking. The company's dressing room was the McBurnie house or sometimes the house across the road, so the dancers might have to wait for cars to pass before they could run across the street to make their cues onstage. Later, as the theatre evolved, and acquired wings, they would use these for costume changes.

Meanwhile, McBurnie raised money – "She would go around pounding the pavement, selling bricks," recalled Julien – and fundraising dinners were also held in the theatre space. McBurnie was invited to numerous diplomats' cocktail parties, and her company was asked to perform when visiting dignitaries were in town. She would then invite her hosts to attend her own functions – in return for a donation. Julien recalls manning the bar on one such occasion: there was no electricity or water, since both had been cut, as the bills had not been paid, and he had to run a hose from a neighbour's house, along with an electric cable for one lightbulb. So the dining space itself was lit by candles, and decorated by McBurnie: "Beryl would do all sorts of things – put a piece of cloth . . . the people loved it." She had a similarly improvised wardrobe: Julien also recalled McBurnie being asked at a party whether she had bought her scarf at Janoura's, then an expensive and fashionable store. "No, no, darling," McBurnie replied. "This is my kitchen curtain." There are anecdotes too about her going to cocktail parties in her nightdress, and improvising a wedding outfit by cutting a hole in the centre of a red satin tablecloth and adding a flamboyant hat.

She spent the money she had saved to buy a car on the theatre. "I said to myself, 'You're a fool, McBurnie. Why do you want a car? What you really want is a little theater. It cannot move you about like a car, but it can move the hearts of so many!'" ("West Indians Gain Respect", *Amarillo Globe-Times*, 20 October 1961, 15). McBurnie never did buy a car, and was notorious among drivers: beware if you saw Beryl standing by the side of the road. If you stopped to give her a ride, she might announce imperiously, "I have to go to Sangre Grande", or, "I have to go to San Fernando" – many miles east and south of Port of Spain respectively – and would insist that her reluctant chauffeur abandon his or her own affairs, transport her to her destination, wait while she did whatever business she had there, then bring her home again (Dr Robert Lee, interview with the author, 2 February 2017).

McBurnie also borrowed her mother's savings, mortgaged the house, and, said the 1961 story in the *Amarillo Globe-Times*, "went about selling her own small paintings to every acquaintance she could buttonhole". She acquired her own house in St James, bought the Roberts Street house and moved out her mother and the other relatives who had occupied it. Finally, 95 Roberts Street was demolished so that the theatre could fill the entire lot. McBurnie persuaded the architect and sometime politician John Humphrey to help construct the new but still rudimentary theatre, along with Julien and another dancer, Earl Augustus. Humphrey not only designed and worked on the building, but also helped clean the toilets and took part in the after-performance dances. Julien recalled, "Christine Millar [a beauty queen of the day], Peter Pitts [later a stalwart of children's Carnival] and Albert Gomes's children came and cleaned this place."

The early dancers describe the first versions of the theatre as resembling a warehouse. It had no proper stage or lights (though George Williams was the official lighting technician). The floor was part wooden, part concrete, and the dancers recalled a show when Julia Edwards's company had to perform on a tarpaulin. Their feet were rubbed raw: "We knew never to dance on a tarpaulin after that," said one. Sometimes they danced in the street, blocking off the crossroads outside the theatre (there is a brief film clip of McBurnie herself dancing there, parading triumphantly in front of the audience). Julien recalls one performance that involved a real pirogue (fishing boat) in the road; he was one of the people who had to heave it in and out of position.

Though it sounds primitive now, the original Little Carib would have resembled some of the calypso tents of the time. There had been theatres in downtown Port of Spain in the nineteenth century, but when McBurnie started staging productions, the only other remotely suitable venue was the Prince's Building, which was not designed to accommodate dance performances or drama; and, in any case, a permanent dance company needed its own rehearsal space, too.

At this point, to its founder, members and fans, the physical infrastructure mattered little. This was just the beginning. As Wilson Minshall said in his contribution to the programme for the 1948 opening, the Little Carib "might well be called 'The Big Idea'. As a building it may not be much to look at, but it is much more than a building. It *is* building. It is the *building* of an art-force. It is . . . binding together many loose ends of cultural aspiration."

The makeshift theatre had a grand opening, on 25 November 1948, with a performance titled "Talking Drums". Minshall was the master of ceremonies, and prominent people who wrote for the programme were McBurnie's former boss, Captain Daniel, the acting director of education; Dr Eric Williams, then a member of the Caribbean Commission; journalist and folklorist Charles Espinet; lawyer Jack Kelshall, on behalf of the Trinidad Youth Council; H.O.B. (Hugh) Wooding, later to become chief justice; and Canon Max Farquahar – all staunch supporters of McBurnie. Williams wrote that her work was significant for three reasons. First, it was a shining light for West Indian women, "who are still so heavily handicapped by their economic status and the traditional conception of the role of women", but whose full contribution was crucial to the future of the region. Second, it was a landmark in the long struggle to encourage local talent which in the past would have had to migrate to find "satisfaction". Third, it represented a conscious effort to develop and expand indigenous culture. Williams added a quotation which later became associated with McBurnie, from the French poet Alfred de Musset, which in translation meant: "My glass is not large, [but] I drink from my glass." Beryl McBurnie drank from her own glass, he said.

The programme for the evening also included the lyrics written by McBurnie for the title piece, "Talking Drums", which was the grand finale and which declared:

Drums!
Do you hear them?
Drums that will talk to you –
Talking Drums . . .
Bringing back a voice –
A voice that speaks of Africa.

The lyrics also made reference to African tribes, to Suriname, Brazil, to Shouter Baptists (whose religion was still illegal under the Shouter Prohibition Ordinance), and to the limbo, bongo and belé dances – all evidence of progressive thinking for the time. As Jack Kelshall wrote in the programme: "At long last some few of our people have reached the point when they are no longer ashamed of their origins."

Other noteworthy items in the show included illustrations of dance techniques from different sources – "Carib, French, African, English, East Indian" – as well as modern dance. There was a "Folk Play"; McBurnie's "Ah Passin", set in a market; something called "Three Peasants"; Indian dances, "Jharoo" and "Massala"; "Tambour Bamboo" (tamboo bamboo, the predecessor of steelband as carnival music, which involved beating differing lengths of bamboo on the ground); the Brazilian song "Terra Seca"; a pan performance by the Invaders "group", led by Ellie Mannette; and, before "Talking Drums", the laying of the cornerstone. This honour went to Wooding; McBurnie's friend the prominent social worker Audrey Jeffers; and American singer Paul Robeson, who was touring the region at the time and whom McBurnie reportedly knew from her New York days. Robeson recited Langston Hughes's poem "Freedom Train", praised the dancers, who "were as good as he had ever seen", and promised to stage *Othello* with the best British and American actors at the Little Carib within a year or two, a promise which unfortunately did not materialize (*CCD*, 32).

Despite this promising start, even by the time McBurnie was interviewed for the *Amarillo Globe-Times* in 1961, the theatre was still only "a three-walled shed with balcony", though the reporter recognized that it was also "a unique institution. It is a magnet which draws top dance talent from all over this big, multiracial island. It also draws clapping, shouting audiences of Trinidadians, foreigners and tourists, including American families connected with the defense base here and the Texaco refinery."

Earl Leaf also appreciated the importance of the theatre, even though the dancers were amateurs: "Out of such enthusiastic local companies are the dances and dance vocabularies of the island rescued from obscurity and eventually brought to the delighted ear and eye of the dance enthusiast everywhere. They are the custodians of the island's rich treasure of dance arts. They do not receive much encouragement from local patrons who could well afford to assist."[45] It was because of this scarcity of support, and because preparations were so haphazard and resources stretched so thin, that there was never enough time to rehearse for shows or make the other preparations that were needed – hence the desperate measures the company sometimes still had to adopt after decades of existence. McBurnie never established a lasting dance school or a substantial body of work, partly because she was too busy doing other things. "Beryl was always begging," explained Ahye. "Whatever we needed, Beryl had to get it."

Luckily for her, McBurnie was hard to resist. Anne Sandfort recalled, "She was bold and commanded attention easily. When she asked a question, it was assertive and she would look you in the face. She could be intimidating." Leaf described her as "a beautiful, intelligent, high-strung Creole girl who is really quite a fabulous person". Even in 1961, the *Amarillo Globe-Times* reporter who wrote about her also obviously fell under her spell, describing her as a "tall, attractive, humorous spinster of indeterminate age, who emanates vitality and radiates affection".

Trinidad occupies relatively little space in Leaf's book, but his photographs include a rare one of McBurnie dancing. She wears a modified douillette that exposes her stomach, and she is spinning, arms outstretched, skirts flying, smiling, but to herself as much as at the audience, caught up in the dance, the music owning her body and soul. The backdrop is the louvred windows of what Leaf described in the caption to another photograph as "the parlor of Belle's quaint and charming Creole home".[46]

But though Leaf was obviously drawn by her attractive qualities, he was not blind to her flaws, and his short account gives a useful and comprehensive picture of McBurnie's personality. He recognized her flighty, whimsical nature: "I won't be surprised to find her huddling round some jungle fire while bevies of naked jungle girls are dancing their rites to pagan gods. Or I may recognize her among the *samba* dancers slithering along the streets of Rio de Janeiro during Carnival." He records that when he asked for help with his book *Isles of*

Rhythm, "Belle", as he called her, "really had no time to act as guest-conductor to visiting firemen what with all her activities on behalf of young Trinidad artists, her political campaigning to elect officials sympathetic to them, her dance classes, the rehearsals for her own repertory company, her researches among the old tomes at the public library, and her field trips to neighboring countries and islands." Nevertheless, she made time for him, although his account also makes clear that the stress of so much activity – and McBurnie's quirky personality – sometimes led to acrimony. He recalls an incident when he and McBurnie almost fell out while dance-hunting (they found performances of the "*belaire*" (belé) and kalinda in "a tiny shack" in Diego Martin, a valley not far west of Port of Spain, then still occupied by agricultural estates). Luckily, he wrote, they had gone with a dancer, Pearl Nunez, so although "Belle was in one of her nervous, fidgety, tempera-mental moods" and he was on edge as well, Nunez's "cool efforts . . . prevented an explosion of violence".[47] For a rela-tively casual acquaintance (assuming that is all Leaf was) to write in such strong terms of a near-quarrel with McBurnie shows how volatile and tempestuous she could be – a trait that over the years was to prove disastrous for the Little Carib.

In another such instance, after her return from a 1940s research trip, McBurnie and Boscoe Holder had a row, possi-bly over the dancer Percy Borde. McBurnie had asked Holder, one of her protégés, to run the company while she was in the United States, and Holder also formed his own troupe, which performed during the war for American servicemen. But according to one source, "Boscoe built his show around Percy, and Beryl reclaimed him. Boscoe's show collapsed. Geoffrey [Holder] wanted to go with Beryl, but Boscoe dissuaded him."

Pearl Primus's biographers say it was Boscoe Holder who discovered Borde and persuaded him to take up dance, but then McBurnie "enticed" Borde to join her company.[48] For that or some other reason, Boscoe bore a grudge against McBurnie for the rest of his long life (1921–2007). Although both Holder brothers began their dance careers with her, she is not mentioned in the biographies of either.[49] Borde left the Little Carib a few years later anyway, after Primus came to Trinidad in 1953 and sought out McBurnie, her former tutor in New York, to help her research Caribbean dance. Primus and Borde, who were both married to other people at the time, fell in love, and he followed her back to New York.

In these early years, as well as bringing into being the physical and creative space of the Little Carib, and helping visiting researchers, McBurnie also continued her own research both locally and around the region. Leaf reports that he "met Belle in Port of Spain, crossed her trail in George-town, British Guiana, met her again in Paramaribo, Nether-lands Guiana [now Suriname], and saw her off to Belem where she intended to study the primitive dances of the Ama-zon River aboriginals". She "had been everywhere", he writes. As for Trinidad, Leaf explains, "For a complete dance record . . . it was necessary to get into the back country beyond Port of Spain where the traditional folkloric dances of the island are performed by the natives."[50] This was where he needed McBurnie's help, so he was able to record how she went about these missions. Other members of the company also went "dance-hunting in the interior of Trinidad", he records, while Boscoe Holder "had just returned from Martinique to bring back the authentic *beguine*".

McBurnie and Holder were Leaf's guides when he went to photograph local dances, staged regularly in villages and some areas of the city itself:

> One afternoon I called for her . . . and we started out of town, picking up Boscoe Holder, gifted young negro pianist, painter, poet and choreographer, on the way.
>
> Belle was in one of her introspective moods that day, so pre-occupied with her own thoughts she never heard my questions. . . . Boscoe knew no more than I. Not until we climbed the Laventille hills did we know our destination and not until she banged on the door of a grass shack and asked the whereabouts of a certain Shango priest did we know the objective of our afternoon's journey.[51]

Laventille, east Port of Spain, had been the home of free African communities before emancipation in 1834 – hence the retention of African practices – but had become a slum area. McBurnie seemed familiar with it, however. They made a long trek through the rain before finding the priest, only to learn there was no Shango feast for another two weeks – too late for Leaf, who was leaving Trinidad soon. So instead, McBurnie, recovered from her moodiness, got some of her dancers to re-enact a Shango ceremony for him; she had seen the dances before and knew them well.

One of McBurnie's later pupils was Anne Sandfort (née Chee Ying), who performed for McBurnie along with her mother Anna Chee Ying (née Deane), who was a pupil and friend of McBurnie's, though not a member of the Little Carib company. Sandfort danced for McBurnie for special occasions from the age of eight, often with her mother, at fundraising dinners at McBurnie's Panka Street home. McBurnie started dance classes there, which young Anne attended every Saturday from the age of thirteen. She remembers McBurnie as "an excellent teacher who . . . demonstrated steps herself. Although she was getting on in age and had curvature of the spine, she was very strong and moved around very quickly and with a sure step!"

Sandfort also has clear memories of McBurnie's approach to teaching dance:

> Beryl always focused on emotions and on telling a story of a multicultural past, African, Creole, Portuguese . . . I remember getting confused because it was very different from the ballet I was also learning. There were no routine steps. However you "felt", Beryl wanted you to express that with movement. She was very dramatic. If she liked what you did, she would turn her head away and hiss. . . . I remember Beryl choreographing a piece to a Portuguese slave song. . . . It was very sad and moving. . . . She did very few pieces herself by the time I came onto the scene and she used other professional dancers like Aubrey Adams and Sonya Moze . . .
>
> She . . . knew who had the passion for it and nurtured that call. Dance always told a story and so it wasn't just about movement, but Beryl made sure we knew what the story of Trinidad and Tobago was, from the slaves to the colonial inhabitants to the street vendors. Everyone had a story and Beryl was the one who knew how to turn these stories into dance.

As a dance mistress, McBurnie was ladylike but firm: she never used bad language, and discouraged her male dancers from doing so. She disapproved of wining, the characteristic sensual hip movement that Trinidadians use in dancing to calypso: her dancers remembered she would say, "Use your hips, but don't wine vulgarly". When a show was coming up, numerous hangers-on would appear at rehearsals, hoping to be picked. McBurnie was kindly but adamant: "Darling, you can't be in the show."

At the Little Carib, McBurnie also designed costumes, painted sets, played the piano, sang and even composed music, among other things. Costumes might be as basic as the theatre itself. "We would use banana leaves or drape ourselves in a length of cloth," recalled Aubrey Adams ("Lady of the Big Idea", *Sunday Express*, 17 October 1993). "Once she saw something that needed fixing, she would fix it," said Bonterre. Although they often had to improvise, she was also a perfectionist: Marquez-Sankeralli remembers going onstage in a costume that had been unstitched, then pinned onto her at the last minute because McBurnie was unhappy with how it had looked.

Although dance was her first love, McBurnie also encouraged other local art forms in numerous ways. She was a very early supporter of the steelband, even though in the 1940s the music and the instruments were not considered respectable, far less art. The bands were regarded as territorial street gangs, partly thanks to the clashes or "riots" between them as they emerged from their respective districts onto the streets for Carnival. In March 1945, McBurnie and the folklorist, singer and actor Edric Connor produced a show for the Trinidad and Tobago Youth Council's inaugural congress at the Prince's Building (Connor had presented shows like this since 1943). They included a steelband which, according to pan historian Kim Johnson, "though unnamed, was probably Invaders". A year later, McBurnie staged a concert of her own at the Prince's Building, and again included Invaders.[52] Thanks to this interest, the governor appointed her to the committee he set up in 1947, at the request of the youth council, to survey the steelbands of Port of Spain and make recommendations to encourage their cultural and recreational potential (Little Carib supporters Canon Farquhar and Lennox Pierre were also on the committee). Invaders, whose panyard was opposite the Queen's Park Oval, literally around the corner, became the Little Carib's house steelband, performing during shows and for the after-show dances. McBurnie was also friendly with Carlton "Sonny" Roach of the Sun Valley steelband from St James, and his band too was sometimes invited to play. So were the Merry Makers (originally Red Army) from Cobotown. The first all-female steelband, Girl Pat, also performed at the theatre and accompanied the dancers on a trip to Jamaica in 1952. And although the theatre was itself perennially strapped for cash, with characteristic generosity, McBurnie allowed it to be used to host a fundraising event to send the first nationally representative steelband, TASPO (Trinidad All-Steel Percussion Orchestra), to perform at the Festival of Britain in 1951.[53]

In 1960, Carlisle Chang designed a Carnival band that came out from Queen's Royal College, the nearby prestige government boys' school. Called Vive la France!, it included pupils from other prestige schools: boys from St Mary's and girls from Bishop Anstey High School and St Joseph's Convent. The band had music by Invaders and choreography by McBurnie, although "We didn't take on the choreography at all," admitted Michael Smart, who was part of the band.

Thus from early on, the Little Carib was more than just a performance space for dance: it was a centre for all sorts of artistic activity, discussion and research, and McBurnie and others used it to foster and encourage other arts and interest in the arts. The artist Wilson Minshall began his piece in the programme for the theatre's opening with the story of a discussion held there some months before titled "The Importance of Being Ourselves". Electric current had gone in Woodbrook halfway through the meeting, so it had to be concluded by the light of a single oil lamp "which was put to the test against the gusty wind", he wrote. Meanwhile, the lights kept coming back for short periods. "It was uncertainty in triplicate – the uncertain darkness, the uncertain floodlights, the uncertain flickering of the yellow flame in the oil lamp."

This was something of an omen. Despite the hard work and the passion that created it, the uncertainty of the Little Carib's existence, its precarious finances and makeshift physical form continued for many years.

FOUR

itting in the auditorium of the Little Carib, Maureen Marquez-Sankeralli reflected, "I don't think there was anybody who became established in folk theatre who didn't pass through here. . . . We were the national dance company."

They were more than that; they were regional pioneers. McBurnie's 1949 show *Gems of the Little Carib*, Eric Williams thought, represented "the principle of self-expression by the West Indian people . . . the cause of the West Indian culture" (*CCD* 39). Describing her influence on Jamaican dance, Rex Nettleford wrote that the Little Carib "served as inspiration. The early Jamaica dance movement dating back to pioneer Ivy Baxter drew on Ms McBurnie's passionate commitment to the notion that there is something called Caribbean Dance." He sums her up as "the earliest pioneer in articulating the Caribbean aesthetic in dance out of Trinidad, Grenada and the Grenadines, where the African presence became the crucible in which the mix of African, Iberian, Gallic and Amerindian cultures merged into a congruent whole".[54]

Though especially intent on reclaiming Trinidad and Tobago's African heritage, McBurnie included every aspect of local culture in her work. "When she did folk shows," Marquez-Sankeralli pointed out, "they represented every nation that lived here: Spanish, African, French, Portuguese".[55] In 1950, for example, McBurnie presented a piece called "Quim Bamba" at the Carnival Sunday night Dimanche Gras show, accompanied by musicians she had brought from the Caura Valley in the Northern Range. For many audience members from Port of Spain, it was the first time they had heard parang, the folk music of Spanish origin brought to Trinidad a century before by Venezuelan *peóns* who worked on the cocoa estates in the hills. (McBurnie had staged a parang show at the Little Carib the previous Christmas, but Dimanche Gras gave it wider exposure [*CCD*, 39].)

In 1950, the British Council awarded McBurnie a scholarship to visit Europe and take a course in physical training methods. During her trip, from September that year, she gave lecture demonstrations and was interviewed by the BBC (*CCD*, 40–41). She met the Trinidad-born pan-Africanist George Padmore, who wrote to his friend the Trinidadian writer Alfred Mendes that McBurnie was "the most interesting woman I have ever met from the W. Indies. For I know only too well the cramp [sic] mid-Victorian atmosphere in which most of our young women still live. It must have required great moral courage on her part to inaugurate the 'Little Carib'. I heard that you did much to encourage her. It is the best cultural effort that London has ever seen from the Caribbean." Mr and Mrs A. Mendes are listed among the "associates" of the Little Carib in the programme for its 1948 opening, and Mendes says in his autobiography that in the 1940s, he wrote reviews and other newspaper articles on topics that included "the Beryl McBurnie *Little Carib* with its significant dance group; and . . . Beryl McBurnie herself".[56]

Nevertheless, that "significant dance group" never had the home it deserved. During the late 1940s and 1950s the Little Carib, still basically a shed, was threatened with demolition several times by the city council. Neighbours complained about it, and it did not have planning permission: McBurnie was asked to submit plans several times, but rarely did so. Thus the *Trinidad Guardian* (16 February 1950) reported that she had been given until 31 March to provide new plans, after missing an October deadline to remove an addition to the theatre. The *Chicago Defender* (15 December 1951, 22) reported that McBurnie was dancing in London with Pearl Primus's company in the West End, trying to raise thirty thousand US dollars to avoid demolition. "I intend to dance myself to a standstill to get the money," she told the interviewer. The following September, still in England, McBurnie told the Guardian News Service she had just heard (again) that the theatre was to be demolished (perhaps yet another council deadline had expired), and was going home immediately to try to save it. She said, "There is nothing I can do about the decision to pull the theatre down, but . . . I shall not spare myself until a new Little Carib Theatre has been built. This time it must be a permanent structure. The theatre represented the cultural side of a West Indies Federation, and it must not be allowed to disintegrate" ("McBurnie to

Return: Plans 'Little Carib 2'", *Trinidad Guardian*, 4 September 1952).

A decade later, it was still being reported that a permanent building was about to replace the rickety structure. The Rockefeller Foundation had invited architect Colin Laird to visit the United States to look at theatre design. Derek Walcott, then working for the *Trinidad Guardian*, wrote in August 1961 that the new theatre would have modern lighting, seating that could be arranged in various ways for up to 480 patrons, and space for "after-show fetes with steelbands and jump-ups". There would still be no room for elaborate scenery, but as the Carib's emphasis, he wrote (with unfounded confidence), was on "experimental theatre and dance", he did not consider that lack of space important. There were grander schemes afoot. "The other functions of the Little Carib, which has been constitutionally revised, include plans for a school, an ethnographic centre for folklore research, the establishment of semiprofessional and drama companies. This is a need which the arduous example of the Little Carib founder, Beryl McBurnie, has brought nearer since she began in the most modest of conditions." Walcott referred disparagingly to the demolition threats, saying McBurnie's company "has acquired the dignity of a national institution and has had resounding successes in Canada, Jamaica and Venezuela". The new theatre would rise on a more suitable site; $250,000 was to be raised by a public appeal. "It will be interesting," he mused, "to see whether the response will be as overwhelming as it has every right to be" ("Unique Lighting Equipment Offered Little Carib", *Sunday Guardian*, 20 August 1961, 15).

It was not; the saga continued. The government did not provide the site, plans to collaborate with the University of the West Indies fell through and no money materialized. The Rockefeller Foundation had been willing to co-operate with Walcott, but its head, who visited Trinidad in 1962, thought McBurnie "mystical, unreliable and not artistically outstanding".[57]

Some of this was not surprising: even her biggest fans found her hard to deal with. She could always rise to a crisis, but could not bear dull routine. On 21 November 1963, Sir Hugh Wooding, chairman of the theatre's board, wrote asking if she were still willing to serve as a director; if so, he begged, would she please come to meetings? For the past year, the theatre had been "more or less in a state of suspended animation. . . . Unless some definite action is taken soon there is a danger that [it] will fall apart through sheer neglect."

In 1964, McBurnie in turn wrote to the board, in a letter that shows the extent of her personal sacrifice. Shortly before, a Little Carib Association had been formed to manage the theatre, but she was in personal financial difficulties as a result of buying her relatives out of the Roberts Street house. With help from barrister and Little Carib stalwart Bruce Procope, she had taken out a mortgage for a house for them for $22,000, but although funds had been found to pay off part, she still owed money on both that house and her own on Panka Street. Her government salary was only $312.73; her mortgage payments were $260 a month. She was not strong enough to organize fundraising shows: "my body has been terribly depleted", she wrote in a letter on 8 July 1964, appealing to the Little Carib associates to discuss the matter in her absence.

The theatre closed in 1965, and in January 1966, Wooding announced a drive to raise fifty thousand dollars, to rebuild it on the same spot. It reopened two years later, but still left much to be desired. Anne Sandfort, a dancer of a later generation, sums up the memories of many patrons even years after that: the theatre was "very dark and hot. . . . There was no air conditioning and the ceiling fans came later. At the entrance there was a small foyer to the right, with wooden benches and a palm tree in the middle. Beryl's sister, Frieda, liked to sit there."

But the Little Carib had nevertheless, as Walcott had claimed, become an institution – as had McBurnie. Decades later, her dancers are still in awe of her. Marquez-Sankeralli says: "She was cultured and highly intelligent. She was very aware of life and what matters. She was never annoyed or vex. She would help to nurse your self-worth." Ron Julien says: "She was such a visionary. It was only as I matured that I realized how brilliant she was." Her friends – and those she influenced – from around the region included Louise Bennett, Ivy Baxter, Nettleford, Alexander Bustamante and Edna Manley.

The significance of the Little Carib Dance Company had been quickly recognized. The dancers performed at the Trinidad Country Club for the cast of the Hollywood film *Fire Down Below*, made in Trinidad in 1956 and starring Robert Mitchum, Jack Lemmon and Rita Hayworth. "They came down with a choreographer from MGM, and took one of our steps," said Hugh Bonterre. The company was invited to perform in Puerto Rico in 1952 at the first Caribbean Festival of Arts. They went to Jamaica in 1955 and to Canada in 1958 and 1959. They were invited to perform for Princess Margaret at the Governor General's House in 1959 (*CCD*, 42, 48, 53, 58). In 1963 and 1964, they performed at the Dimanche Gras shows produced by Errol Hill, and in 1965, McBurnie choreographed Hill's play *Man Better Man*.[58]

The breadth of McBurnie's knowledge of regional dance, drawn from her research, was also acknowledged. She never wrote much, although, in 1958, she produced a thirty-one-page booklet called *Dance Trinidad Dance: Outlines of the Dances of Trinidad*, with forewords by Philip Sherlock of the University of the West Indies, Mona; Hugh Wooding; and Walcott. In it, McBurnie told a three-page "Story of the Dance", about the varied origins of Trinidadian dances, followed by sketches of dancers and step-by-step instructions for dances, including the limbo, shango, "ghadka" (gatka) or East Indian stick dance, and one called "The Arawaks". A typical set of these instructions, for the bongo (how useful they might be to later choreographers is debatable) begins: "1. Rocking horse movement right foot in front left close together – Girls opening and closing skirts. 2. Cross left then right foot in front, point heel to side. 3. Cross right over left using heel to stamp with hop." But for the two 1943 "soundies" showing McBurnie dancing, there are very few other surviving records of her choreography.

McBurnie lectured at a symposium in 1963 along with theatre expert Errol Hill, anthropologist J.D. Elder, Derek

Walcott, and artist and theatre and Carnival designer Carlisle Chang.[59] She addressed Trinidad's dance heritage, declaring that in the region it "would not come lower than third if one were to assess which territory had made the greatest contribution in the field of dance, owing to its varied ethnic heritage". The main thrust of her talk, summed up in the published proceedings,[60] was the question: "Are we prepared to accept what is originally ours, and not be afraid because it is simple and given to cottons and no silk? Or are we afraid because most of the vital expression of our folk material is of African origin?" She spoke authoritatively of the many dances derived from these traditions, and her dancers demonstrated them, from three "Arawak" dances that "celebrated, in ideal form, the vanished reality", to Venezuelan, French and British (though she dismissed the British influence as minimal), Chinese, Portuguese and Indian, while she stressed, "The most significant element in West Indian dance is the African."

The unnamed writer who summarized McBurnie's apparently ad-libbed talk added:

> In answer to questions at the end of her lecture, Miss McBurnie said that in her view dance was the most significant West Indian art form since it contained the greatest variety of raw material waiting to be worked on and presented. She agreed that this raw material needed more elaborate choreography than it had so far received. There was a lack of creative talent in the West Indies, because so many of our most gifted dancers had to go abroad if they wished to earn their living as dancers.

The inclusion of "Arawak" dances sheds some light on McBurnie's technique and attitude to choreography. It was not just a matter of reproducing identically the original folk forms – obviously, in the case of the dances of the First Peoples, this was impossible. Asked in 1981 about the loss of authentic traditional dances, she replied, "That must happen . . . some of the authentic forms are bound to be affected. . . . The modern world is more interested in entertainment than in authenticity." In addition, the dance could not remain static, frozen in time, because: "It's now been injected by a lot of modern dance movement, ballet movement. You must expect that: people are going for training around the world and coming back. So there's a greater development of folk dance, a greater variety of expression and movement."[61]

One change, which McBurnie herself pioneered, was the blend of dance and theatre. As Hugh Bonterre put it: "She was the first person to make the symbolic marriage between dance and drama" – a marriage that had inspired Walcott in 1957, when he met McBurnie and her dancers at a summer school at the extra-mural studies department of the University College of the West Indies in Mona, Jamaica. Errol Hill and Louise Bennett-Coverley taught drama; Ivy Baxter taught West Indian folk dance; and McBurnie modern creative dance. Walcott saw in McBurnie's work a way to use folk material to create authentic West Indian theatre. His *Ti-Jean and His Brothers*, which is based on St Lucian folklore and incorporates song, dance and dialect, was written shortly after this.

The Little Carib Company performed in the 1958 festival of the arts for the inauguration of the Federation of the West Indies, for which Walcott wrote the pageant *Drums and*

Colours, staged in the open air in the Botanical Gardens in Port of Spain. The dancers rehearsed for the Little Carib production, *Binaka*, in the Hollows, across the road in the Savannah. There were frequent crises. Doing a last-minute check, McBurnie discovered the piano was waterlogged. So she and Aubrey Adams flagged down a stranger driving round the Savannah, went to Woodbrook, somehow manoeuvred the Little Carib piano on top of the good samaritan's car, tied it down and got back to the Botanical Gardens just in time for the pianist to begin playing the introduction while the piano was being wheeled onto the stage. Maureen Marquez-Sankeralli remembers running up the steps to the stage, slipping because they were wet, and cutting her leg. McBurnie hastily wrapped the bleeding wound with a piece of cloth and told her, "Maureen, you've got to go." Maureen climbed the steps again and arrived onstage on cue.

The production got standing ovations, but mixed reviews. A British critic writing in the *Trinidad Guardian* said McBurnie's company "gave an exotic, well staged and colourful pageant of West Indian history in dance", but the second part "was spoiled by the Portuguese dance, which lacked enthusiasm, and the British dance, which was appalling . . . her African Dance was magnificent" (*CCD*, 60).

By 1959, Walcott had moved to Trinidad and was holding weekly drama workshops at the theatre. The Little Carib Theatre Workshop gave its first performances in 1962, and he wrote that the company hoped to inspire the same "interest in drama as there is in dance at this theatre, and is experimenting with the possibilities of fusing the two into an indigenous West Indian form". He had come to Trinidad in July with the St Lucia Arts Guild, which presented his *Journard* and *Malcochon* and four of his twin brother Roderick's plays. McBurnie "rather uncertainly" told Walcott's biographer that it was the difficulties the Walcotts encountered on this visit that led her to invite Derek to form a theatre workshop at the Little Carib. But the irascible Walcott and the imperious McBurnie proved an unstable, explosive combination. This was apparent as early as 1962, in the actors' first production. Bruce King records in his book about the Theatre Workshop, "Unfortunately Beryl McBurnie and Walcott were quarrelling then, as often; McBurnie purposefully flushed the toilet of the Little Carib in the middle of [Samuel Beckett's] *Krapp's Last Tape*."[62]

Walcott, who wrote about the arts for the *Trinidad Guardian*, was sometimes scathing about dance performances at the Little Carib; perhaps McBurnie felt he was biting the hand that fed him. In an annual theatre roundup, for instance, he singled out "two major disasters", one of them the Little Carib's "hastily executed *Serenal*, a re-hash of better days" (*Trinidad Guardian*, 1 January 1961, 7). Even his praise was not always undiluted, as in his review of the 1962 pre-Carnival production *Quibamba*:

> Miss McBurnie has choreographed several new dances, not all of them realized in the under-developed outlines of her narrative. A "Chinese" number, featuring Maureen Marques, generates an echoing stillness at points, but seems basically rootless and blurred. It is, despite these, an achievement for the dancers, since it indicates the reserve that lies behind the enameled sur-

face. The same is true of the pointlessly revived standby, "Spanish", which gets weaker every season, and "Aborigines", which has grown looser since I last saw it.

An aesthetic graph of most Little Carib dances would be very jagged indeed – perhaps inevitably, since Miss McBurnie is forced to make handouts to her audiences to keep the houses full. When she does this with native wit, as in the hilarious, poker-faced and puppet-rigid "Moko" and "Nègre Jardin" dances, the result is exhilarating. These are regional dances, however, and need a bolder clarity of gesture or a rigidity of narrative line that would deepen their meaning. She concedes a large slice of "The Twist" to the public, but it is an interminable slice, and it weakened the general impact of the show on Tuesday night. (*Trinidad Guardian*, 1 March 1962, 5)

King says the exact cause of the final break between the Little Carib and the Theatre Workshop in 1965 is uncertain.

McBurnie was unhappy with the kinds of experimental plays Walcott was producing. The actors were taking more and more Little Carib time for rehearsals, using the Little Carib for drama, whereas McBurnie saw her theatre as primarily for dance . . . A dispute about when the Theatre Workshop could rehearse is said to have become a heated argument about Walcott and the actors not paying their dues or some rental to the Little Carib, after which the actors arrived one evening and the door of the Little Carib was locked; they had to find a new home.

The actors, who eventually became the Trinidad Theatre Workshop, did not have a stable base for many years. Eventually they resumed staging productions at the Little Carib, but it was never their home again. When they organized a season of dance and drama there in 1974, it was pointed out (in an unsigned article in the *Tapia* newspaper, possibly by Walcott himself) that this was the first theatre season at the Carib in over a decade.[63]

Ron Julien and his wife at the time, Margaret Roebuck, restarted the Little Carib as a theatre in the late 1970s, renting it out, as there was no resident dance company. "We tried to get Beryl to relaunch one, but it never happened," he recalled. "We told Beryl, 'Do the choreography, we'll manage the theatre.' We had hoped Astor Johnson would take over as choreographer, but he had his own company, though he danced with the Little Carib company."

In 1982, the Little Carib faced a new threat, when McBurnie took umbrage at the way it was being run. A *Sunday Guardian* headline on 7 February announced: "Little Carib Coup". For the previous two years, the theatre had had a full-time manager, the Irish-born Helen Camps, who had acted with the Trinidad Theatre Workshop and set up a production company, All Theatre Productions, to provide technical support for drama. When Camps had appeared in Jean Genet's *The Maids* in 1977, going offstage meant walking out of the Little Carib onto White Street, as the stage had no real wings. While she waited, straining her ears for her cue, McBurnie appeared. She walked down the street and asked Camps where she could buy a chicken (it may not have been by chance, or in innocence, that McBurnie was there on such a bizarre quest and felt it appropriate to distract Camps). After this surreal encounter, Camps went back onstage, but all through the rest of the play she was thinking, "Something has to be done about the infrastructure." So she did it. Under her management, the Little Carib acquired carpets and cushions, sponsors and patrons, and though Camps was not paid for her work, the theatre became financially viable for the first time (Judy Raymond, "Moving Spirit of Theatre's Shining Moment", *Sunday Guardian*, 3 June 2001).

McBurnie, while given due respect and invited to every production, was not involved in the day-to-day running of the theatre. Now she complained that dance had virtually been banned from the Little Carib at the expense of drama – the "coup" referred to in the headline. McBurnie insisted dance must come first, and recalled the years she had spent walking the streets of the country begging for funds for the theatre. "It is a folk theatre for the dance," she insisted, "and I want to see the Little Carib operate as it was originally intended, free from encumbrances and undue influence so that the people of Trinidad and Tobago and the Caribbean can share in the facilities and development of theatre which is truly a product of our own indigenous efforts." She ignored the legal and organizational framework of the Little Carib, which by then did not belong to her alone, though a new company was still to be legally incorporated so that the theatre could acquire charitable status. Its treasurer, Emile Elias, noted that thanks to Camps, it could now pay all its expenses. Another board member, Selwyn Ryan, pointed out that Camps incorporated folk elements into the Carnival musicals that her company staged. Ryan also observed that McBurnie's accomplishments were due to her personal charisma, not her organizational skills; and that the theatre was now an institution in its own right, no longer dependent on its founder. All this drama was played out in the media. McBurnie remained unmoved, taking what she felt was the moral high ground in insisting that the theatre must be true to the original vision – hers. She denounced a recent production, the Carnival folk musical *A Nancy Story*, by Elliot Bastien, which in her eyes had used "the language of the colonial slavemaster, of the merchants and planter class" (*Sunday Guardian*, 28 February 1982).

Camps resigned on 1 April, and a new board was formed, consisting of McBurnie, Aubrey Adams, Elias, William Massiah, Ron Julien and Margaret Roebuck (*CCD*, 114–20, 130). For McBurnie, it would be a pyrrhic victory. The unsigned *Tapia* story of 1974 had observed that partly because local audiences always wanted something new, many of the best dances of the past by McBurnie and others had been lost. Audiences were not entirely to blame for this, however. There had long been signs that McBurnie was being stretched too thin. As early as 1949, Albert Gomes had written: "Many of McBurnie's dance creations have failed to satisfy, because of the impression they convey of having been hastily improvised and not fully worked out. They seem like mere fragments placed into programme pattern by an imagination too casual and furtive to sustain and co-ordinate its efforts . . . many of her dance creations have been weak in dramatic structure and, therefore, artistically unsatisfying" (quoted in *CCD*, 36).

McBurnie never did have the time to focus on creating dance. According to an interview in the *Amarillo Globe-Times* (20 October 1961, 15), having been made director of dance by the government in 1950, she was still working as a physical education instructor at no fewer than four teachers' colleges, "chasing back and forth between courses in ethnic dance. This leaves only evenings and Sundays – and barely enough energy – for her life work". Her big project for the following year was "a folk opera combining drama with music and dance, to be called 'Chiki Chong,' a native word for 'a kite, a bird, or a sprightly little man,' as a symbol of the islands". McBurnie also taught classes in San Fernando, where she had formed the Arawaks dance group in 1955 (*CCD*, 56); and ran the junior troupe, the Humming Birds, at the Little Carib. Then there was travel and fundraising.

In any case, while undaunted by emergencies and brilliant at improvising in a crisis, McBurnie did not have the self-discipline or patience to run a dance company, holding classes week after week. She did not have business skills, despite her relentlessness when it came to raising money. Sometimes senior dancers kept the company going while she was away or busy with other work. But they were steadily leaving. Over lobster at the Hotel Normandie (McBurnie did not usually eat that well, she confessed), she claimed she was not troubled when her best dancers left. "Their going away doesn't vex me. I want to spread good ethnic dancing as far as possible."

"But wherever they go," wrote reporter Betty Reef (*Amarillo Globe-Times*, 20 October 1961, 15), "it is her own flaming enthusiasm transmuted into motion (she disturbs and communicates joy at the same time, a friend said) which produces their electrifying performances." These "electrifying performances", however, were not being danced at the Little Carib.

In the end, this steady haemorrhaging of the best dancers – and potential choreographers, managers and dance mistresses to lead classes and rehearsals – proved fatal. Percy Borde went off to New York to marry Pearl Primus, though he returned occasionally and gave classes at the Little Carib. Kelvin Rotardier also went to New York, becoming a principal dancer and choreographer with the Alvin Ailey American Dance Theater, then founder and head of the Ailey Student Performance Group. Marquez-Sankeralli was a professional dancer and choreographer in Toronto. Jeff Henry won a Rockefeller Scholarship, then went to Canada as a choreographer and university lecturer. Owing to a combination of this attrition, the fact that McBurnie's energies were expended on other things, and her autocratic temperament, by 1970 there was no Little Carib Dance Company, though occasional shows were staged. (McBurnie herself stopped dancing in 1972, after the *Dingolay* production of that year, her dancers recall.)

McBurnie had said in the 1961 interview that most of the support for the Little Carib had come from overseas. Certainly if Eric Williams, who became prime minister shortly after, had offered material and not only moral support for her work, she could have channelled more energy into creating dance, rather than begging for money to build and repair the theatre and pay for sets, lighting and the myriad other costs of productions. It was no wonder that at times even the dauntless McBurnie sounded a little bitter. Asked at Carifesta in Barbados in 1981 whether the revival in regional and local folk dance was the culmination of the work she had done, she replied, "Everyone knows the government took the Little

Carib's work and put it in Better Village." This was the Prime Minister's Better Village Competition, an annual festival, begun under Williams's prime ministership (1962–81), in which communities from around Trinidad and Tobago perform folk dances and skits. McBurnie's feelings were echoed by Marquez-Sankeralli: "Now cultural performances get government support. They took her work and get credit for it." Her former dancers are understandably resentful that performers who followed the trail they blazed got government support, whereas cash for the Little Carib always had to be painfully and time-consumingly scraped together by McBurnie and others. Among the few personal papers in the Beryl McBurnie Collection are a number of letters asking for sponsorship and receipts for corporate donations for cans of paint and other such minor items.

Nevertheless, McBurnie received an award at Carifesta in 1981, and was touched by it, though she focused on the recognition of others. "George Lamming spoke, and I was extremely thrilled to hear his interpretation of what the Little Carib meant. Edna Manley got an award too; she inspired me a great deal in her life. And Sparrow: he is really the bard, he makes statements all the time . . . he's not afraid to be very articulate as regards what should be said [about political events]." McBurnie was modest about whether the Little Carib had influenced other countries. "I do not know," she said, but then recalled the 1957 seminar at the University of the West Indies in Jamaica: "Other islands came up to Mona and some said it was the first time they had ever been exposed to the folk culture of the Caribbean. So perhaps they might have been." Nor did she take all the credit for the formation of the Little Carib, but remembered it this way: "A group of people decided we were going to stick together in a theatrical movement. There was conviction, there was beauty, there was order. . . . People came from all over the world, fascinated by our dances." When the company toured overseas, she recalled, audiences were fascinated by "our vigour, artistry, beauty".[64]

Nevertheless, it was McBurnie who was rightly showered with honours. As well as those from dance companies she had inspired, she was awarded the Order of the British Empire in 1959; two national awards from Trinidad and Tobago – the Humming Bird Gold Medal in 1969 and the country's highest award, the Trinity Cross, in 1989; and an honorary doctorate from the St Augustine campus of the University of the West Indies in 1976. There were numerous anniversary celebrations at the Little Carib, with performances by distinguished dancers and musicians, and programme notes by no less prominent writers.

And yet, over thirty years after she had set up the theatre – the most tangible and durable aspect of her life's work – television interviewer Bruce Paddington of Banyan Television[65] pointed out that the Little Carib was still "in a bad way". Was she distressed by that, after seeing the "splendid facilities" in Barbados? "Certain drawbacks still remain with us," McBurnie replied blithely, "but the years will deal with that." The theatre would somehow acquire better lighting, sound equipment, air conditioning, "with time". "I'm not jealous," she added. "I feel the Carib will come into its own." In

Trinidad, she explained, it took a great event to make things happen. She believed Carifesta would be that great event: "After this, the government – there will be a volcanic eruption – the government will be very thoughtful, there will be a change of heart, I'm sure about that." Perhaps she hoped a Carifesta held in Trinidad (which did not happen until 1992) would galvanize the government into bringing the Little Carib up to standard. In fact, McBurnie believed governments all over the Caribbean, and particularly in Trinidad and Tobago, would think: "The time is now; we can't keep back the culture any more."

But the fact was, over four decades since she had begun working to build respect for local culture, she still had to say, "It will take some time, but we'll eventually get there."[66]

FIVE

The Little Carib Theatre was not McBurnie's only concrete contribution to the arts. Having turned her family's house into the theatre, she converted her own home at 34 Panka Street, St James, into what she hoped would become a training centre for it: the Folk House.

Like the Little Carib, the Folk House was "opened" many times. There was an event, *L'Ouvert*, on 1 December 1981, which included Aubrey Adams as master of ceremonies, Margaret Walcott as house manager and décor by Peter Minshall. Artist Pat Chu Foon was also credited, and the evening was dedicated to the memory of Sir Hugh Wooding, who had died in 1974. Among the notable performers were Jerry Jemmott on flute; singer Fritz Nothnagel-Gurley; an ensemble doing an East Indian dance; designer Geoffrey Stanford, acting on this occasion; Nadine Mose, who danced ballet professionally in New York; Torrence Mohammed, by then leader of the Arawaks dance troupe of San Fernando; and a finale that included the Village Drummers, a resurrected Little Carib Company (some of them also now distinctly veterans), and McBurnie herself. A programme for another show, ambitiously titled *From Columbus to Now*, was also filled with well-known names as performers and technical crew, and also listed "opening art courses": classes by Maureen Sankeralli in tai chi; drama by Sonya Moze and Errol Sitahal, "among the best Directors in Trinidad today"; dance by Astor Johnson, "undoubtedly the finest creator of Folk Dance in this country"; and other leading practitioners of drama, dance, music and art.

Four years later, in an episode of the television show *Gayelle*, interviewer Errol Sitahal reported that McBurnie was "opening another one of her homes into a performance area and museum". The Folk House was "opening" again, as a way of attracting publicity and hopefully funding. McBurnie told viewers it was called the Folk House because "it is for folks", and was envisaged as an arts training centre because there was none; she had decided to devote her own house to this use, as she was hardly at home. "I have at the back of my mind to get a dance company eventually," she added.

She gave Sitahal a tour, explaining the purpose of the rooms, each dedicated to a supporter.[67] A performance space was named after Albert Gomes, "who fought the council tooth and nail so they didn't throw down that building" – the theatre – when it was threatened with demolition. The foyer was named after Canon "Maxie" Farquahar, also a newspaper columnist. "With his pen every Sunday he would fight for us and eventually we won and are still in existence." The main auditorium honoured Wooding, who only ever missed one board meeting and made possible the company's tours to

Jamaica and Canada. A stage area was named for Audrey Jeffers; the theatre used to hold fundraising concerts by neighbourhood children for her Coterie of Social Workers. The music room was for musician Marjorie Padmore, head of the National Cultural Council. The library was dedicated to Eric Williams, and McBurnie talked about their relationship:

> I knew him from my student days at the Government Training College: when C.L.R. James left for London, he took his place. I recognized a strong nationalist, who was interested in the culture of the West Indies. He had a strong interest especially in music.
>
> He gave away his salary, he never had money. You would tell him a sad story and he'd give it to you.
>
> He always felt the Little Carib was not well treated. . . . He would organize functions, take us to Manzanilla [Beach] in his big Buick, hold social evenings at his own home. . . . He always told me to get serious about my work.

The balcony was dedicated to Olive Kelshall of the Methodist Church, one of McBurnie's teachers. "She taught us a lot about Christianity. Jesus said, 'Love one another as I have loved you,' and my love has been illustrated in giving these two buildings to the country." The museum was named after Marie Solomon, one of her teachers at Tranquillity. Even the spiral staircase was dedicated: to Barney Maurice, former dancer and choreographer, who would contribute to Little Carib events out of her own pocket.

McBurnie had selected these friends because they had influenced her and because "I bear a grudge that we in Trinidad do not pay enough attention to our heroes. They are the people that will give Trinidad life". Framed photos decorated the spaces named after these heroes, amidst the artefacts in the museum – a mortar and pestle, carved African chairs, an old-time wooden ice-cream churn, lengths of tamboo bamboo, stacks of papers, a collection of books – and McBurnie's own household goods, among the black-painted and curtained stage and other areas earmarked for artistic activity. Her life was, as always, quite literally arranged round the theatre. Seated on moth-eaten cushions or in a bentwood rocker, McBurnie is smiling and serene, her optimism undimmed after all the years of struggle and apparent lack of progress. The ten-year-old Folk House was not finished, she admitted, insisting, "But it's a workable idea" ("Lady of the Big Idea", *Sunday Express*, 17 October 1993).

The Folk House was not as spacious or as grand as McBurnie's account suggests; she was perhaps describing her ultimate vision for the building rather than the reality. Anne Sandfort remembered what it was actually like: "The inside was converted to a theatre. As you entered, there was a bar on the right, open space in the centre for chairs and a stage. Stage left led to the infamous kitchen. Stage right led to a small room with an array of old gowns. . . . She did not have a bed. She slept on a chaise longue that was in one of the small rooms that ran along the side . . . completely surrounded by old gowns and costumes. . . . She quite often would leave the door open and liked to watch from her chaise longue as you entered and she would not reveal where she was until she felt she had observed you enough. Everyday life was a theatrical opportunity for Beryl." McBurnie later had the jalousies at the front replaced with louvred doors that opened directly onto the street, so that the pavement could be used as a performance space too.

She lived alone in that house for many years. McBurnie never married; it was often said she was married to her work, although some of those who knew her say she must have had lovers. "You can't be married and do work," she said ("Lady of the Big Idea", *Sunday Express*, 17 October 1993). Anne Sandfort remembered McBurnie saying the headtie she often wore was "very important because the number of knots tied, indicated whether you were single or married. My mother asked her which was it for her. She giggled but never responded. She never spoke of her love life, past or present. Dance was Beryl's life. I never encountered anyone more committed." In 1961, McBurnie told an interviewer: "Work is the most important thing in life. Love is secondary – only a long goodbye" ("West Indians Gain Respect", *Amarillo Globe-Times*, 20 October 1961, 15).

When Felipe Noguera, who became a protégé, friend and collaborator, met McBurnie in the mid-1980s, she was no longer officially involved in the Little Carib and was trying to establish the Folk House. Ron Julien and Margaret Marquez were running the theatre, though McBurnie was "angling to get back in".[68] She asked Noguera to teach at the Folk House, and he gave martial-arts, dance and drama classes there for several years. At that time she was still choreographing herself, mainly for children, at the Saturday "enrichment programme". She would help with the plays he directed, and was also busy rounding up donations of food for fundraising events.

Noguera says they became very good friends, even "soul-mates". "She was like my adoptive mother. We were very close. I think of her every day and miss her all the time. . . . She was delightful. She enriched my life in so many ways." He remembers McBurnie as charming and attractive, but very sensitive; she would become agitated if someone was not fully committed to a task: "I worked with her, fell out with her, made up with her many times. You had to subordinate your own will and ego to hers, you had to sift through the precious gems she had. People would say, 'That's a crazy old lady', but she had a brilliant mind. It was worth it to sit at her feet." Despite her wilfulness, she was gentle and compassionate, he said, recalling President Ellis Clarke saying in a speech at the Folk House that McBurnie's grace was the perfect companion to her humility. She had progressive political views, but was more bourgeois in her tastes. She was difficult to manage. She was commanding and compelling – but with "a very sweet way of begging". Noguera retold a well-known anecdote about a bandit who broke into McBurnie's house while she was there: in his version, not only did the thief apologize, but she even got him to clean the house.

Noguera spent a lot of time with McBurnie looking back at her life and work:

> Her career took her well beyond Trinidad and Tobago and the Caribbean – her research, her work – but she wasn't able to transcend it, to look at it objectively, she was very immersed in it. But that was also her greatest strength: she never lost the common touch, her love and empathy for this culture, her grounding.

> Beryl was a fighter. She had an ability to stand up and fight for this country and this culture. She was indomitable: apart from her genius as an artist, her patriotism was exemplary. Amerindian, Chinese, French, Spanish – she loved them all. She embraced the country as a whole, with all its strengths and weaknesses.

McBurnie would reminisce about the early years: conversations with Eric Williams; C.L.R. James recruiting her to stage presentations for federation and independence; her friendship with Norman and Edna Manley; her role in fostering Rex Nettleford. She spoke of James teaching her at Tranquillity and directing her in Molière's *Dancing Master*. She recalled her New York days, talking of the time when, she claimed, she studied under Melville Herskovits (the anthropologist who wrote *A Trinidad Village* with his wife Frances); replacing Carmen Miranda; seeing Paul Robeson as Othello; and, in Trinidad, her expeditions with Andrew Carr, especially to the Rada community, whose dances she then staged.

She was upset with Harry Belafonte (who had two hit calypso albums), believing he had used some of her music without acknowledgement, Noguera said – a claim still echoed bitterly by some of McBurnie's dancers (his 1957 "Cocoanut Woman", credited to Lord Burgess and Belafonte, was said to be a version of her "Plantain Woman", for instance); but she was not resentful. "She had a lot of love in her heart." Likewise, Noguera said she did not harbour animosity towards Boscoe or Geoffrey Holder. She was disappointed not to be asked to run the Best Village programme, a task given to Joyce Wong Sang (Eric Williams's sister-in-law), but Noguera eventually concluded it was just as well: "She couldn't deal with the tedium of organizing and managing needed to run Best Village."

In her later years, McBurnie went on organizing variety shows: dancer/choreographer Sonja Dumas, who had gone to her lecture-demonstrations as a teenager, remembers choreographing a duet in 1998.[69] Dumas and her dance partner, Gregor Brady, went to the Folk House to perform it for McBurnie, who watched from her chaise longue, apparently indolent, until she saw something she did not like: "You have no idea how sharp her eyes would be," Dumas recalled. "She would say, 'No, no, no . . . do this more . . .' She would become the director." Dumas was disconcerted when McBurnie decided at the last minute that the piece – set to classical music, at her request – needed a prelude danced to African drumming, but added it anyway: "There was no saying no to her."

McBurnie also held soirées at the Folk House for many years, even though sponsorship was becoming scarce and organizing them became too much for her. Anne Sandfort, who performed at them with her mother, recalled the distressing details in a blog post:

> One occasion would be Ballet, another African and another Classical Indian. The dinner parties were a disaster behind the scenes though. Beryl was a hoarder and the kitchen was the worst you have ever seen. She had an elderly maid, who had a limp and, well, she needed help herself. . . . So my mother would always go to Beryl's house early to help . . .

> The sink was always filled with black water. I kid you not; and the mountain of used dishes, months old and covered in fungus and decay, piled from corner to corner.[70]

McBurnie visited old friends and protégés, but was housebound for some time before her death. As well as Noguera, Aubrey Adams, former dancer and chairman of the Little Carib, spent a lot of time with her. She received a monthly allowance from the state, according to Adams, as well as a grant of fifty-four thousand dollars to repair her house (*Trinidad Express*, 31 March 2000). Noguera remembered discussing her legacy just after the great calypsonian Lord Kitchener died in February 2000. McBurnie expected her time to come soon – she was right: she died the following month. Her will, made the previous year, directed four trustees, including Adams, "to help build managerial capacity and hopefully, to be of one heart and mind for the maintenance of good order and astute governance of the 'to-be-incorporated-company' . . . the Little Carib Theatre and Folk House".

McBurnie, who was eighty-six, died of old age, Noguera believes, "though there was some broken-heartedness in it". She had two carers, one of whom in particular, Esther Springer, ensured she did not suffer a lot. But at the end, according to Noguera, McBurnie was "pursued by ghosts", an experience she found distressing. "She would say, 'But I don't want to go anywhere.' I tried to calm her down: I would say, 'If it's time for you to go, you've had a good life; we're like your children, we'll take care of your interests.'" He saw her the day she died – 30 March 2000 – and later got a call from her carer. McBurnie had been declared dead after being taken to the nearby St Clair Medical Centre.

Her funeral on 6 April 2000 showed that while the institutions McBurnie set up might have languished, her efforts had not been forgotten. Her funeral was at the Anglican Holy Trinity Cathedral in downtown Port of Spain, a bigger venue than the Tranquillity Methodist Church. Not only her family, friends and former pupils, but politicians and other artists also attended. The Invaders steelband played for her, of course. Rex Nettleford – by then head of the Jamaica National Dance Theatre Company and vice chancellor of the University of the West Indies – flew in to pay public tribute to her. "If Beryl hadn't existed, it would have been necessary to invent her," he began. "But luckily for us, she invented herself." His eulogy combined truthfulness and tact, touching on the qualities that both helped and hindered her successes. He spoke of her "self-assertion", which he said was made necessary by the nature of the society in which she lived. And he hinted at her scattiness – perhaps exacerbated by her taking on single-handed so much of the work of the Little Carib – speaking affectionately of her "creative disequilibrium", and "the madness in her method" (Judy Raymond, "Beryl Would Have Liked This", *Trinidad Guardian*, 7 April 2000, 2).

Methodist minister Sheldon Dewsbury admitted he had not known McBurnie, but summed up her life's work accurately when he said, quoting the Bible, "She has done what she could." The Lydian Singers choral group sang the "Hallelujah Chorus" for her; Noguera sang too – "Terra Seca", the

Brazilian song McBurnie had long loved, and which had been on the programme when the Little Carib was opened fifty-two years before. Some of her former dancers performed for her one last time, among them Maureen Marquez-Sankeralli, Molly Ahye and Carol la Chapelle. After the two-hour service, her body was escorted out of the cathedral with tassa drumming, moko jumbies, a dance by schoolchildren and African drumming, en route to her burial at the Lapeyrouse Cemetery.

In the years since the rift at the Little Carib, the theatre companies that had used it had found other spaces. For a while Helen Camps had her own Tent Theatre – literally a tent, in a grassy space next to the zoo; later, one of her protégés, Raymond Choo Kong, ran the Space Theatre, at Bretton Hall, Victoria Avenue, above the bar that had housed Walcott's Theatre Workshop after McBurnie had put them out years before. Many dance companies took to using the more capacious Queen's Hall. The Central Bank Auditorium, which was not designed for theatre, but which was air-conditioned, became the venue of choice for several years, and other, more comfortable theatre spaces came and went. As a result, although theatre was eventually allowed back into the Little Carib, often it was dark.

In 1988, the theatre had marked its fortieth anniversary; the programme includes a poignant prayer by Margaret Marquez-Roebuck, who had danced there with her sister Maureen. She wrote:

> The Little Carib Theatre looks forward
> With God, in the hope that one day we will acquire

A proper lighting system
A proper sound system
Adequate seating
Air conditioning along with sound proofing etc.
But with all these dreams we hope never to lose
The Spirit of the Little Carib.

Eventually some of those hopes were realized. In 2006, the government promised the theatre an annual grant of one hundred thousand dollars, through culture minister Joan Yuille-Williams, who had once danced there under McBurnie; only one instalment materialized, however. In 2007, the government promised four million dollars, which the board estimated was the cost of restoring and upgrading the theatre, but only half the funding was received initially, so work stopped for some time. Architect Sean Leonard rebuilt the exterior, raising the roof and removing the old breeze blocks that had let in the sounds of barking dogs, passing traffic and Invaders practising around the corner. The auditorium was enclosed and air-conditioned, as were the new dressing rooms. There was equipment for recording shows, a new box office and a spacious lobby, featuring sliding windows to let in the night breeze; on its walls hang numerous large photographs of McBurnie in her prime. The funds were not enough to complete the job, but the Little Carib reopened in June 2011. Since then more work has been done, such as reupholstering the seats (though they are fixed, so the auditorium cannot be reconfigured for theatre in the round, as in the past).

The theatre stages an annual tribute to McBurnie, around the time of her birthday on 2 November. There have been other tributes, too: Dumas choreographed a piece for the Animae Caribe animation festival in 2011, "Belle Rosette", danced to music by Gary Hector of the local rock band joint-pop. She later expanded it into a quartet, performed by dancers with their faces covered in fabric, so that rather than looking like individuals they would invoke the spirit of music – or of McBurnie.

Once again, theatrical productions are staged at the Little Carib – whose sole income is from rentals and ticket sales of its own productions. For a few years the Trinidad and Tobago Film Festival used the theatre for screenings. Some dance companies still stage annual seasons there, and in November 2016, a twelve-member resident company, the New Little Carib Dance Company, gave two inaugural performances in McBurnie's honour. Panman Ray Holman also performed. In an interview in the *Sunday Express* (6 November 2016), the company's artistic director Andre Largen said, "Because of her we are. And because of what she planted we can grow. I cannot fill her shoes, but I can stand on her shoulders. Her dream continues, through these young dancers."

The Folk House did not fare so well. Under McBurnie's will, the trustees were to incorporate a new company to run both the theatre and the Folk House: the latter was to house a library and a rehearsal space that could be rented out. But by the time her will was probated, the Folk House, uninhabited since her death, had fallen prey to thieves and vagrants, explained Mike Germain, who took over from his cousin Ralph Rollock as company treasurer in 2005 and chairman in 2008. McBurnie's awards were stolen from the house after her death. Thieves ripped out plumbing fixtures and left the pipes leaking, so that much of the building and its contents were irreparably damaged by water. Then, on 16 September 2016, it was demolished. The house was not protected under National Trust legislation, and the board had sold it earlier that year because it was beyond repair, even if there had been funds to restore it. The city corporation had complained frequently about the rats and weeds that took over the house and the land on which it stood, and the company could not afford the upkeep.

The board stipulated that any new building on the site should bear a plaque saying it had once been McBurnie's home. Before it was knocked down, former dancer Ron Julien and Little Carib operations manager Trevor Jadunath borrowed an army truck and packed up what books and papers could be salvaged. There was a lot of material: Anne Sandfort remembered: "Beryl was a hoarder. She kept every magazine, article, costume from everything she did." Over thirty boxes – most full of books – were sent to the national library to become a special collection. But almost all the surviving material is badly damaged by water, insects and neglect, and it is possible that these brittle, flaking volumes, the last remnants of the Folk House, may not be salvageable.

It is a magpie's collection. It includes a few personal letters, and programmes from productions at the Little Carib and the Folk House, as well as one from "All as One", a children's rally for the queen's visit in 1966, in which McBurnie was involved, and from local and overseas shows she had seen. There are books on dance (including several on Martha

Graham, and Geoffrey Gorer's seminal *Africa Dances*), mythology and the arts, some of which she must have collected during her travels in Spain, France and Germany. But much of the material must have been intended as the basis for the Folk House library. Some may date from McBurnie's own childhood, such as the sets of classic nineteenth-century novels. There are schoolbooks with various children's names in them; Marlowe and Shakespeare, Milton, Tennyson, Keats; texts of local plays and several copies of anthropologist J.D. Elder's *From Congo Drum to Steelband* (1972). Two dozen volumes of *Histoire Générale de l'Eglise* are interspersed with magazines on Eid-ul-Fitr; Reader's Digest almanacs; C.L.R. James's *Party Politics in the West Indies*; and Hitler's *Mein Kampf*, in German.

There is a scrapbook containing inspirational handwritten quotes from the romantic poets, and, tucked into it, a handful of cards and letters sent to congratulate McBurnie on good shows or on her Order of the British Empire in 1959, and copies of a few letters to and from friends. There are one or two worm-eaten notebooks in which she scribbled on-the-spot observations on local dances, but the oil from the ball-point ink has made the paper translucent and the writing almost illegible. She made notes for the opening of Carifesta, the sporadic regional folk arts festival that started in 1972: she wrote to a friend in 1991 that she had been asked to design an opening ceremony for it (Carifesta V was staged in Trinidad and Tobago from 22 to 28 August 1992). A notebook titled "Carifesta: Suggestions" detailed her hopes for the festival, such as making the Caribbean "an ever present reality in the minds of its peoples – and unity in diversity". Hope no. 6 (she listed 1–2, then 4–7) makes a declaration which could have been the motto for McBurnie's own life: "The end of thought is action."[71] In the November 1991 letter, to an unnamed woman friend she called "Meh zwee",[72] who was out of the country, she wrote, "So you have gone. . . . And I am sure you would not be surprised to learn, that I too want to go!!!!!!!" She explained, "It is like hell here." Yet McBurnie could still find reason to be optimistic. She set down her vision for the Carifesta launch, with Trinidad ringed by a series of beacons to be lit by a relay of runners, and bells "pealing throughout the land" the theme of *Pictures at an Exhibition* (she wrote out the first line of the score); and argued, "If the government is sensitive, they would realise that as Trinidad is slowly dying, there is a great opportunity to save it, via 'CARIFESTA', God knows." She never lost her faith in the redemptive power of art and the oneness of the Caribbean people.

There is a poignant moment in the 1981 television interview at the Barbados Carifesta when McBurnie says urgently, "Things are slowly coming our way, but they're not coming fast enough, because we would like to see it happen before we die. Art and culture are the expression of a culture, it's through art and culture that we can see the spirit, whether it is alive and meaningful or dead."[73] When McBurnie says "before we die", she means "before *I* die". What she was hoping for did not happen; apart from the predictable belés and limbo of Best Village, and the same troupes and artists being sent to successive, occasional Carifestas, Trinidad governments' main artistic focus is Carnival. By contrast, McBurnie praised the Cuban contingent, which she said was the finest exponent of art she had seen, attributing its success to state support:

> The government decided it had better take the medium of art to express the Cuban way of life. It's not so in the West Indies. . . . Outside Jamaica, the other West Indian islands have not analyzed what art can do to a country or for a country, and so they have been a bit amiss. All these years we have been trying to make the government take the vehicle of art and culture, make the country a finer place to live in.

And yet, asked in 1993 if she had any regrets, she replied, "I don't think so. Sometimes I get mad about it . . . but somebody had to do the work." She did that work as long as she was physically able. As to why she persevered, the reason, she replied – as though surprised the question needed to be asked – was: "The life itself, my darling. You have to keep pushing and prodding, you have to keep nourishing it – it's like watering a plant. You have to *keep at it*, because as you get careless the weeds take over" ("Lady of the Big Idea", *Sunday Express*, 17 October 1993).

In her last years, McBurnie was "melancholy, though not bitter", recalled Noguera. "She didn't like the direction the country was going in, but she didn't lose faith." She would say that what "poor little Trinidad" needed was "not a higher standard of living but a higher quality of life. She lamented the iconoclastic, ephemeral nature of a society that would throw away the marvellous creations built every year for Hosay and Carnival."

Noguera believes the story of McBurnie's life should be taught in schools and children should do projects on her life and work for their exams. "We should revamp the curriculum so Beryl and people like her are not only known, but revered. . . . She should not be allowed to be forgotten."

Meanwhile, the Little Carib still stands, in better physical condition than ever; more importantly, it has a special place in the hearts and the memories of the artistic community. As well as dance and drama, it has always been a home for poetry readings and music. It was the venue for André Tanker's public debut with his band, after McBurnie heard them playing at the home of John "Buddy" Williams (Tanker and his own band later provided music for many shows there). Tanker never forgot that it was at the Carib that he first heard Andrew Beddoe, master drummer and Orisha priest, and began to understand the African roots of Trinidadian music. It was through his connection with the Little Carib, too, that Tanker met Walcott and began composing and performing music for his plays.

Ray Holman, arranger for the Starlift steelband, was introduced to the instrument at twelve, in 1956, when he and his friend Roy Rollock, McBurnie's nephew, tried out some pans at the Little Carib: in those days their families would have disapproved of steelbands, but the Little Carib was more respectable. (Both later joined Invaders, however.)[74]

As it was for them, the Little Carib was part of masman and artist Peter Minshall's boyhood. His father, the artist Wilson Minshall, who worked for the Tourist Board, was an early supporter and often served as master of ceremonies at the theatre. So Peter was "a little adopted son of Miss Beryl's".[75]

He had finished studying and was working in theatre design in London when McBurnie called him, saying she was in London to put on a show and he had to help her, since his father and brother had helped her in the past. She was raising funds, as ever – "buying bricks to build a theatre" – as Minshall put it; and wanted him to design some Amerindian bird costumes for her. He used the same cane and hessian he had used for the wings of his first, victorious Junior Carnival Queen hummingbird costume in 1974. McBurnie's London show was at the Commonwealth Institute, and began with nine dancers processing onto a circular stage. Minshall remembers McBurnie's last-minute intervention as she rushed to the venue in a taxi, carrying pots of pelau to feed the cast: she stopped the taxi to pick nine bare black twigs from Hyde Park, and told him each dancer must carry one as she walked onstage. "It was one of the most beautiful theatrical images I've ever witnessed," he recalled. "In the midst of all the madness, the now-for-nowness of us shines."

Minshall returned to Trinidad to design a Carnival band for Stephen Lee Heung in 1976, the iconic Paradise Lost, and in 1978 McBurnie let him use the Little Carib as the mas camp to produce the costumes for the first band he brought out under his own name, Zodiac. He returned to post-independence Trinidad, he remembered, "at a point when we were wondering, 'Who are we ? . . . We want to mean something'", and McBurnie encouraged him in that quest, as she did his friend and fellow artist the late Pat Bishop. In turn,

CHAPTER FIVE

Minshall helped design some of the productions McBurnie staged at the Folk House.

A later generation was also nurtured at the Little Carib. The rapso group 3canal put on its annual pre-Carnival shows there, until it outgrew the venue. Though 3canal now has its own performance space, Wendell Manwarren, band member, actor and drama teacher, considers the Little Carib "our home, where we all grew up in the arts" ("State-of-the-Art Little Carib Reopens", *Trinidad Express*, 5 June 2011).

The lawyer and trade unionist Jack Kelshall, a staunch supporter of McBurnie, was prophetic when he wrote in the programme for the opening of the theatre in 1948: "Had the fight not been bitter then perhaps 'The Little Carib' might have been built like any other building – out of wood and stone and iron only. Perhaps it would have forfeited that permanence which is reserved for things of the spirit and which is bought by pain, and which will preserve 'The Little Carib' and the idea it houses long after ordinary buildings have crumbled into ru[s]t and rubble."

McBurnie's legacy has always been far more than the bricks and mortar of the theatre. "Beryl inspired us all," said Aubrey Adams, an early devotee. "She lectured us on the arts, on morals, values. She had a library. She got her supporters to come and visit us" ("Lady of the Big Idea", *Sunday Express*, 17 October 1993).

That legacy extended far beyond Trinidad and Tobago, too. In 1978, McBurnie was celebrated in New York when the Alvin Ailey Dance Company marked its twentieth anniversary. She was hailed as a pioneer of black dance, along with Pearl

Primus and Katherine Dunham (*CCD*, 110). Regionally, in 1987, celebrating its twenty-fifth anniversary, Jamaica's National Dance Theatre Company honoured three "high priestesses of Caribbean Dance" – Ivy Baxter of Jamaica, Lavinia Williams of Haiti and the United States, and McBurnie; they were flown to Jamaica for the occasion. McBurnie is one of the people to whom Rex Nettleford's book about his company, *Dance Jamaica: Renewal and Continuity*, is dedicated, and he pays further tribute to her in the text, naming her as a seminal influence on the early dance movement in Jamaica.[76] The inscribed copies of his books that he sent her are among the Beryl McBurnie Collection housed in the Heritage Library, Port of Spain.

McBurnie devoted her entire life to the Little Carib and what it represented: the preservation of authentic West Indian dance traditions – and in that she succeeded. Her dedication to what was at the start a solitary vision cost her what might have been long-term fame and financial security in the United States, and certainly a comfortable old age; she poured all her own money into the theatre and its productions, as well as spending endless time and energy raising funds from elsewhere. She never really retired – from choice, working as long as she was able to keep the theatre and its traditions alive. She achieved what Kelshall had described as "that permanence which is reserved for things of the spirit and which is bought by pain". There was indeed pain, and disappointment, but there was far more. McBurnie found many friends, allies and helpers along the way who shared her vision. There were moments of despair, but she retained the endless optimism that sustained her for decades. Her achievements were recognized. She was part of a generation of strong women who overcame the prejudices of their time to stamp their mark on Caribbean history, and her willpower and quirky personality were celebrated and loved. As Eric Williams said, she drank from her own glass. Beryl McBurnie lived the life she chose.

NOTES

1. "Footprints", in the DVD *Beryl McBurnie: Pioneer of Caribbean Dance*, produced by Banyan Ltd, Port of Spain (n.d.).

2. Interview with former Little Carib dancers Ron Julien, Maureen Marquez-Sankeralli, Yvonne Sandy and Hugh Bonterre, Little Carib Theatre, 1 February 2017. Unless otherwise indicated, all quotes from these dancers are from this interview.

3. Nettleford, *Dance Jamaica*, xiii.

4. Ahye, *Cradle of Caribbean Dance*, 2. Hereafter cited in the text as *CCD*.

    In her booklet *Trinidad Carnival and Dance* (apparently a programme for some unspecified event in aid of the Little Carib), McBurnie says it was after she staged a production at the Empire Theatre in 1940 that "a group of dancers was formed, and from then on the dance of Trinidad and Tobago had taken root". The Coralita Club: McBurnie, "Little Carib" (in the programme for the 1968 reopening of the Little Carib).

5. Information on the Rollock family from interviews with Michael Germain, 13 and 23 October 2017; email from Vanetta Rollock Gittens, 16 October 2017; and Rollock family tree, courtesy Michael Germain. On William Rollock teaching Beryl about music: Pierre, "Beryl McBurnie and the Little Carib".

    The houses on Roberts Street may have been renumbered at

some point: the Little Carib is now number 95, but many people refer to it as number 69 (for example, McBurnie, "Little Carib and West Indian Dance").

6. James, *Minty Alley*, 24.
7. James, *Beyond a Boundary*, 24; 29–30.
8. Williams, *Inward Hunger*, 35.
9. Ibid., 37–38.
10. Ibid., 35.
11. Gomes, *Through a Maze of Colour*, xii.
12. Calder-Marshall, *Glory Dead*, 252.
13. Grant, *Negro with a Hat*, 53, 254.
14. Calder-Marshall, *Glory Dead*, 126, 250.
15. Stone, *Theatre*, 24.
16. Dudley, *Music from Behind the Bridge*, 86–87.
17. The Radas maintained (and maintain) the cult of Dangbwe, a serpent god of Dahomeyan origin. Andrew Carr later wrote a monograph on them.
18. From programme notes for *King Jab Jab*, directed at the Little Carib by Helen Camps (1981).
19. Gomes, *Through a Maze of Colour*, 85.
20. Ibid., 82. Shouter Baptism is a syncretic Afro-Christian faith whose practitioners are known as "Shouters" because of their shouting when they "catch the spirit" – that is, experience spirit possession. This was frowned upon by colonial authorities, especially as some of their ceremonies and rites were practised in the open air. The faith was outlawed in 1917; this ban was not repealed until 1951. "Shango" was the term used at the time for the Orisha faith, an Afro-European syncretic religion that combined Yoruba and Christian elements. Shango is the Orisha (god) of iron, symbolized by a double-headed axe.

   Portuguese workers were imported from Madeira after emancipation to work in the cane fields as labourers (although they proved unsuited to the task and soon left, often to set up small shops). Thus although fair-skinned, they were not regarded as white in terms of class in their early years in Trinidad. Gomes himself was raised and lived for a long time in the working-class district of Belmont.

21. De Verteuil, *Trinidad*, 178.

22. Details of some of these dances were recorded in Trinidad in books by European residents, paintings from Dominica and neighbouring islands by Agostino Brunias and the lithographs made in Trinidad by Richard Bridgens.

23. Anne Sandfort, email to the author, 2 February 2017. Unless otherwise indicated, all quotes from Sandfort are from this correspondence.

24. The soundies are included on the Banyan Ltd DVD *Beryl McBurnie*.

25. Gérard Besson, interview with the author, 30 January 2017. Unless otherwise indicated, all quotes from Besson are from this interview.

26. Ahye cites this passage as being from a 1977 book or memoir by McBurnie called *Trinidad and Tobago and Dance*. I have been unable to trace this publication.

27. Pierre, "Beryl McBurnie and the Little Carib", 7.

28. Cook[e], "Just on the Program", 11.

29. Ahye was a longtime disciple of McBurnie, becoming a member of the Little Carib company in 1952 and a principal dancer until 1965. The book is based on Ahye's thesis for her master's degree in performing arts.

    The American photographer Earl Leaf, who visited Trinidad in 1948, gave an account of McBurnie's New York sojourn that he must have got from her: he also says she taught West Indian dance at the New Dance School in 1944 (*Isles of Rhythm*, 176).

30. Beckford, *Katherine Dunham*. Dunham was born in Chicago between 1909 and 1912. She trained as an anthropologist and did graduate work with Melville Herskovits, later one of the co-

authors of *A Trinidad Village*. She also danced while at university, and got a grant to do field research in 1935 on Caribbean dance and ritual, which she incorporated into her work as a choreographer. Another Dunham dancer, Lavinia Williams, wrote to *Dance* magazine that she "was told" Dunham had taken lessons from McBurnie (*Dance*, December 1966, 35; cited in *CCD*, 4).

31. Schwartz and Schwartz, *Dance Claimed Me*, 34–35.
32. Ibid., 3, 119.
33. Cook[e], "Just on the Program".
34. Schwartz and Schwartz, *Dance Claimed Me*, 35.
35. Cook[e], "Just on the Program".
36. Schwartz and Schwartz, *Dance Claimed Me*, 253. Calypso, originally sung in French patois, is in fact generally considered in Trinidad to be African in origin.
37. Cook[e], "Just on the Program".
38. Dudley, *Music from Behind the Bridge*, 92n3.
39. Cook[e], "Just on the Program".
40. Schwartz and Schwartz, *Dance Claimed Me*, 119. It must be remembered that Boscoe Holder and McBurnie fell out during the 1940s and never reconciled, though he remained a friend of Frieda; Boothman's view of McBurnie was almost certainly coloured by that of her elder brother, as powerful and combative a personality as McBurnie herself.
41. Funk, "Beryl McBurnie".
42. Information gathered from interviews by the author with former Little Carib dancers Ron Julien, Maureen Marquez-Sankeralli, Yvonne Sandy and Hugh Bonterre, Little Carib Theatre, 1 February 2017.
43. Leaf, *Isles of Rhythm*, 182.
44. Michael Smart, interview with the author, 9 February 2017. Unless otherwise indicated, all quotes from Smart are from this interview.

45. Leaf, *Isles of Rhythm*, 182.
46. Ibid., 179. Anne Sandfort described the house at Panka Street; her account suggests Leaf was also describing and photographing the original Panka Street house before McBurnie remodelled the exterior as well as the interior. "She had lovely jalousie windows at the front and hanging baskets of flowers and plants. The inside was converted to a theatre."
47. Leaf, *Isles of Rhythm*, 176, 186.
48. Schwartz and Schwartz, *Dance Claimed Me*, 127.
49. For the absence of any mention of McBurnie from the Holder brothers' biographies, see MacLean, *Boscoe Holder*, and Jennifer Dunning, *Geoffrey Holder*. According to the latter, Boscoe simply created his own dance troupe in 1947.
50. Leaf, *Isles of Rhythm*, 174.
51. Ibid., 176.
52. Johnson, *From Tin Pan to TASPO*, 82; (Connor's shows), 190. See also Dudley, *Music from Behind the Bridge*, 87, for a similar account of the later shows, though with slightly varying dates.
53. Johnson, *Tin Pan to TASPO*, 211, 312n39, 247, 251.
54. Nettleford, *Dance Jamaica*, 12, ix.
55. McBurnie was concerned with West Indian folk dance, but was not averse to setting it to the European classical music she would have learned as a child: her *Folk Fantasy* ballet, which included characters such as douens and Papa Bois, was set to parts of "William Tell", and elsewhere she used music by Wagner (*CCD*, 44–45).
56. Mendes, *Short Stories*, 214–15; Mendes, *Autobiography*, 132.
57. King, *Derek Walcott*, 195.
58. Banham, Hill, Woodyard, *Cambridge Guide*, 240.
59. McBurnie, along with C.L.R. James and Eric Williams, introduced Chang to folk culture; he went on to become a mas-band designer, painter and muralist, and designed the Trinidad and Tobago coat of arms.

60. McBurnie, "West Indian Dance", 50–54.
61. Banyan Ltd, *Beryl McBurnie* (DVD).
62. King, *Derek Walcott and West Indian Drama*, 24–25, 43.
63. Ibid., 49, 217.
64. "Footprints", in Banyan Ltd, *Beryl McBurnie* (DVD).
65. Interview at Carifesta, Barbados, 1981, ibid.
66. "Footprints", ibid.
67. Interview at Folk House, December 1985, ibid.
68. Felipe Noguera, interview with the author, 31 March 2017. Unless otherwise indicated, all quotes from Noguera are taken from this interview.
69. Sonja Dumas, interview with the author, 13 October 2017. Unless otherwise indicated, all quotes from Dumas are from this interview.
70. Anne Sandfort, "La Belle Rosette", *Cowbird* (n.d.), http://cowbird.com/story/83466/La_Belle_Rosette/.
71. McBurnie may have been thinking of Carlyle's "The end of man is action, and not thought" (*Sartor Resartus*, [London, 1893]).
72. The endearment refers to a small black bird also known as a cici zeb.
73. Banyan Ltd, *Beryl McBurnie* (DVD).
74. Dudley, *Music from Behind the Bridge*, 165.
75. Peter Minshall, interview with the author, 26 October 2017. Unless otherwise indicated, all quotes from Peter Minshall are from this interview.
76. Nettleford, *Dance Jamaica*, xiii, 12.

BIBLIOGRAPHY

Ahye, Molly. *Cradle of Caribbean Dance: Beryl McBurnie and the Little Carib Theatre*. Port of Spain: Heritage Cultures, 1983.

Banham, Martin, Errol Hill, George Woodyard, eds. *The Cambridge Guide to African and Caribbean Theatre*. Cambridge: Cambridge University Press, 2004 [1994].

Banyan Ltd. *Beryl McBurnie: Pioneer of Caribbean Dance* (DVD). Port of Spain: Banyan Ltd, n.d. [the most recent item in this collection is dated 1991].

Beckford, Ruth. *Katherine Dunham: A Biography*. New York: Marcel Dekker, 1979.

Calder-Marshall, Arthur. *Glory Dead*. London: Michael Joseph, 1939.

Cook[e], Marvel. "Just on the Program but Belle Rosette Reveals Rare Keen Artistry". *New York Amsterdam Star-News*, 7 June 1941.

De Verteuil, Sir L.A.A. *Trinidad: Its Geography, Natural Resources, Administration, Present Condition, and Prospects*. London: Cassell, 1858.

Dudley, Shannon. *Music from Behind the Bridge: Steelband Spirit and Politics in Trinidad and Tobago*. Oxford: Oxford University Press, 2008.

Dunning, Jennifer. *Geoffrey Holder: A Life in Theater, Dance, and Art*. New York: Harry N. Abrams, 2001.

Funk, Ray. "Beryl McBurnie: The Flowering of La Belle Rosette". *Caribbean Beat* 94, November/December 2008.

Gomes, Albert. *Through a Maze of Colour*. Port of Spain: Key Caribbean, 1974.

Grant, Colin. *Negro with a Hat: The Rise and Fall of Marcus Garvey*. London: Vintage, 2009 [2008].

James, C.L.R. *Beyond a Boundary*. London: Serpent's Tail, 1994 [1963].

———. *Minty Alley*. London: New Beacon Books, 1975 [1936].

Johnson, Kim. *From Tin Pan to TASPO: Steelband in Trinidad, 1939–1951*. Kingston: University of the West Indies Press, 2011.

King, Bruce. *Derek Walcott: A Caribbean Life*. Oxford: Oxford University Press, 2000.

———. *Derek Walcott and West Indian Drama*. Oxford: Oxford University Press, 1995.

Leaf, Earl. *Isles of Rhythm*. New York: A.S. Barnes, 1948.

MacLean, Geoffrey. *Boscoe Holder*. Port of Spain: Aquarela Galleries, 1994.

McBurnie, Beryl. *Dance Trinidad Dance: Outlines of the Dances of Trinidad*. Port of Spain: Little Carib Theatre, 1958.

———. "The Little Carib and West Indian Dance". In *Foundation Stone*. Port of Spain: Little Carib Theatre, 1968.

———. *Trinidad Carnival and Dance*. Trinidad: Little Carib Theatre, n.d.

———. "West Indian Dance". In *The Artist in West Indian Society: A Symposium*, edited by Errol Hill. Port of Spain: University of the West Indies Department of Extra-Mural Studies, n.d. [c. 1963].

Mendes, Alfred H. *Short Stories, Articles and Letters*, edited by Michèle Levy. Kingston: University of the West Indies Press, 2016.

———. *The Autobiography of Alfred H. Mendes 1897–1991*, edited by Michèle Levy. Kingston: University of the West Indies Press, 2002.

Nettleford, Rex. *Dance Jamaica: Renewal and Continuity: The National Dance Theatre Company of Jamaica 1962–2008*. Kingston: Ian Randle, 2009.

Pierre, Rose Ann. "Beryl McBurnie and the Little Carib: A Woman and Her Achievements". Caribbean Studies Project, University of the West Indies, 1978.

Sandfort, Anne. "La Belle Rosette". http://cowbird.com/story/83466/La_Belle_Rosette/Accessed 15 March 2017.

Schwartz, Peggy, and Murray Schwartz. *The Dance Claimed Me: A Biography of Pearl Primus*. New Haven and London: Yale University Press, 2011.

Stone, Judy S.J. *Theatre: Studies in West Indian Literature*. London: Macmillan Caribbean, 1994.

Williams, Eric. *Inward Hunger: The Education of a Prime Minister*. London: Andre Deutsch, 1969.

ACKNOWLEDGEMENTS

First I must thank Shivaun Hearne of the University of the West Indies Press for commissioning this book, for allowing me extra time to finish it when other projects got out of hand, and for being a lovely editor to work with.

For moral support and cheerleading I am grateful to Andrew Mitchell, QC; Dr Kim Johnson; Marlon Rouse; and my children Justin and Dr Luke Raymond-Guillen and Saskia Johnson.

The real beginnings of this book go back many years, and I am indebted to Lennox Grant for his guidance and visionary leadership as Trinidad *Sunday Express* editor in the 1990s, when I first wrote about Beryl McBurnie and other theatre practitioners. The late Molly Ahye was also crucial to the original profile I wrote of McBurnie: as well as a helpful interview, she also gave me a copy of her book *Cradle of Caribbean Dance*, a vital source of documentary material about McBurnie's work.

I would also like to thank the efficient and knowledgeable Jasmine Simmons and other staff of the Heritage Library, National Library, Port of Spain for allowing me access to the yet-to-be-catalogued Beryl McBurnie Collection there.

A special debt of gratitude is owed to the indefatigably enthusiastic and helpful Ray Funk, who passed on his collection of newspaper clippings from McBurnie's "Belle Rosette" years in New York and beyond, and kindly gave me access to his archival photos of her from that period. Christopher Laird of Banyan Productions gave me a copy of an invaluable set of video recordings of interviews with McBurnie and the "soundies" of her dancing as "Belle Rosette" in New York in 1943. Dr Robert Lee provided suggestions and introductions as well as giving me an interview. Dr Kim Johnson lent me some of the essential books I needed for research.

I am also grateful to the people who knew Beryl McBurnie and granted me interviews and insights into her character, career and context: Anne Sandfort, Charlene Rollock, Felipe Noguera, Gérard Besson, Michael Germain, Michael Smart, Peter Minshall, Dr Robert Lee, Sonja Dumas, Trevor Jadunath, Vanetta Rollock Williams; and some of the still-devoted dancers who worked with Beryl McBurnie in the early years: Hugh Bonterre, Maureen Marquez-Sankeralli, Ron Julien and Yvonne Sandy.